The challenges of life, as ＿＿＿＿＿, ＿＿＿＿＿, ＿＿＿＿＿ put you on top. In *Called to Be Different*, you will find the story of one who was taken under yet came out victorious. On the other side of struggle, you will find a compassion for those still defeated. The compassion of the author leaps from the pages. The deeper you are in hurt, the louder these words will ring true, binging the sound of freedom to the hurting and setting them free.

—Evangelist Roger Webb, Orlando, Florida

In *Called To Be Different*, Joyce Howard presents her journey of faith as a response to the call God has communicated to her over the years. She puts her call with previous experience in a sequence that portrays a journey that is continuing today. It is an insightful window into her passion to follow the Lord while walking according to a different "drumbeat." It is interspersed with simple, obedient steps in response to the word of the Lord and her understanding of Scripture. The book is a pleasant instruction for all of us to respond to the same call she has. We are truly *Called to Be Different* so that we can communicate a different message to the world. It is a call to freedom to be like Jesus.

—Pastor James Solomon, Living
Waters Chapel, Caro, Michigan

Called
to be
Different

Joyce A. Howard

A Woman's Journey into the Heart of Christ

Called to be Different

TATE PUBLISHING & *Enterprises*

Published by Tate Publishing & Enterprises, LLC
127 E. Trade Center Terrace | Mustang, Oklahoma 73064 USA
1.888.361.9473 | www.tatepublishing.com

Tate Publishing is committed to excellence in the publishing industry. The company reflects the philosophy established by the founders, based on Psalm 68:11,
"The Lord gave the word and great was the company of those who published it."

Book design copyright © 2010 by Tate Publishing, LLC. All rights reserved.
Cover design by Tyler Evans
Interior design by Nathan Harmony

Published in the United States of America

ISBN: 978-1-61566-413-9
1. Religion: Christian Life: Inspirational
2. Religion: Christian Life: Personal Growth
10.01.07

Dedication

This book is dedicated to all the members of my family—my children, grandchildren, sisters, brothers-in-law, nieces, and nephews—whose love gives meaning to my life. It is dedicated to the future generations of our family, for whom I pray daily. And, most of all, it is dedicated to the Lord Jesus Christ. His continuous presence, love, and guidance are the motivating forces of my life.

Acknowledgments

I have been privileged to have the support of several individuals in the completion of this book. Thank you to Edie Zalewski, Joe and Pat Weinburger, Mark Howard, Kaye Campbell, and Betty Sagash for patiently reading through various drafts of the book and offering their wise advice. Thank you to Karen S. Williams for so graciously offering her editorial help and writing the foreword. Thank you to Pastor James Solomon, Dr. Robert Koch, and Evangelist Roger Webb for reading the book and giving it their endorsement.

Thank you to Stacy Baker, Amanda Reese, Tyler Evans, and Nathan Harmony from Tate Publishing for their help and assistance in the completion of this book.

My husband, Ted, was diagnosed with MS (multiple sclerosis) in September of 1987. The last day he was able to work was in May of 1991. I started my teaching job at a community college in September of 1991. By the fall of 1992, Ted had broken his hip and was never able to regain mobility. Thus began a series of hospital stays. While at home, Ted required twenty-four-seven care. Our families and friends made up the bulk of that care network, most notably Ted's sister, Riky, and her husband, Jack. Part of my teaching load was to teach night sections that kept me from home until eleven o'clock. One or two nights a week, Jack would drive from work for the two hours that it took him to get to our home. Another part of my teaching load was all-day Saturday labs. Riky and Jack came to stay with Ted on those Saturdays.

Along with teaching, I took part in state and national conferences. I had to be assured that Ted would be in good hands while I was out of town. More than once, Paul, one of Ted's brothers, made the trip from Toronto to stay with him. Ted's brother Pete also came from across the state to help.

My family was part of this care network as well. My sisters, Deb and Pat, came to help. Pat's husband, Ron, came from work to spend afternoons caring for Ted. My nephew Randy helped with Ted's care for a couple of years. Various nieces helped.

Friends were part of his care network. Tammy, Rose, Sue, Diane, Tonya, Becky, and Rosemary were mainstays of Ted's daily care. Without the love, care, help, and support that our families and friends gave to us, we never could have survived through those fourteen years (1991–2005).

I acknowledge and thank each of these people from the bottom of my heart.

Without the help and encouragement of those mentioned—and so many more—I would not be where I am today. Thank you!

Contents

Foreword

Loss is an unsettling, seminal event that cannot be escaped in the lives of most women. It is known by so many names. The demise of a parent or child. Watching the love of your life choose another and walk away. Debilitating sickness. Divorce. Lost confidence or hope. The death of your husband, your most intimate and trusted confidante, lover, and friend.

For women who fail to see loss as an invitation to journey, the grief that follows can be protracted, devastating, even bearing heart-rending physical symptoms: heartache, tears, depression, throbbing headaches, and an inability to sleep or eat. Excessive grief can even yield deceptive spiritual wounds that urge a woman to become suicidal or cry out, "Why have I been abandoned by God?" Yet for a petite, Midwestern professor named Joyce, a fiery Christian woman with a radiant, angelic smile—a smile as dazzling as her heart—the loss of her second husband,

Ted, became an occasion for her to not let grief turn her glory into shame. Instead, she learned at Christ's leading just how fearfully and wonderfully made she really was, and that embers of life yet to be lived stirred in mourning's disesteeming ashes.

Called To Be Different: A Woman's Journey into the Heart of Christ, by Joyce A. Howard, invites women who have experienced traumatic loss and grief of any kind to learn that through God's richest grace, they are equipped to journey toward the heart of Christ, to accept his call to be different, strong. Wise enough to see promise and his promises beyond tears. Smart enough to encourage others to hear his gracious call. Listen. Can you hear it? He is saying, "Rise! Be free! I have called you to be different. I have called you to be wonderful, extraordinary, pleasant, and pleasing. I died for you to overcome death. Death, where is your victory? Where is your sting? Weeping may endure for a night, but joy comes in the morning."

—Karen S. Williams
Author and Poet[1]
Inkster, Michigan

Introduction
God's Call to Us

Each of us walks a unique path in this life. Just as each of us was uniquely created by our Father God, each of us has been given a unique path in life. My experiences within my family have been different from those of my sisters. The experiences of my son and my daughter are different from me.

Uniqueness is not a mistake, nor is it a coincidence. Uniqueness is God's purpose and plan. As we look at the world around us, we see that no two leaves or snowflakes are alike. God intentionally created uniqueness. It is so important that we understand this foundational principle of our Creator—the ultimate artist of the universe.

When we lack this understanding of God's design, our tendency is to judge others from our personal viewpoint. We judge based upon our personal struggles, experiences,

Called to Be Different

and limited knowledge. I have been guilty of this very sin: judging the others in my life. One of the greatest lessons I have had to learn is to let go of the desire to judge and allow myself to be free of the need to control my world by placing limits on those around me.

God's call to us is one of forgiveness, reconciliation, and healing. This is the story of one such journey—mine. From the onset, let me be clear that *it is a journey that is still in progress*. I expect the process will not be complete until I stand before our Lord and Savior Jesus Christ.

It has taken me most of my life to be able to receive God's forgiveness. You may wonder why that would be so. It has been my inability to understand my need to repent, including what to repent of, how to fully repent, and how to fully accept the Lord's forgiveness. How we as humans view sin and how God views sin are not necessarily the same. Often our view of sin has more to do with prejudice, bigotry, and self-righteousness than it does with the things the Lord views as sin. I will attempt to explain this.

Throughout his Word, God teaches us about repentance, forgiveness, and reconciliation. He has made it very clear that reconciliation comes only through his Son, Jesus Christ. Many of us have been caught up in other experiences similar to the experiences that Job went through in his life. For me, it took a crisis in my life to finally reach a point where I could cut through the stockpile of accumulated hurts, lack of understanding, false information, etc., that were keeping me from truly hearing the gospel message of the Lord's salvation.

The good news is that the Lord was waiting at the other

end of my struggle to greet me. He was waiting there with open arms to welcome me into his kingdom, the kingdom of his unfailing and fathomless love and acceptance. He was waiting to pour forth his Spirit on me so that I was not simply "born again" and left without direction but endued with his power that is transforming my life. That transformation continues to be a work in progress.

In this book I will share painful experiences from my life. I do not share them to draw attention to myself nor to gain sympathy. I share them in the hope that others will progress through areas of hurt within their own lives. For these, there is an answer: Jesus Christ.

I have learned that emotional hurts cannot be ignored. I tried for many years to push the hurts down and ignore them. But the Lord would not let me leave them that way. Why? Because we cannot grow in our Christian walk until we let go of those weights that are holding us back.

Some of the hurts I will share have to do with my family, especially my parents, both of whom I have loved totally and completely my entire life. I have many wonderful and happy memories of our family life, but these are not what the Lord has quickened me to share. Perhaps someday the Lord will give me the opportunity to write about those happy times. Both my parents have gone to be with the Lord. They are dearly missed by my sisters, by me, and by our children.

Some of the hurts I will share have to do with decisions I made during my life. Even after accepting Jesus Christ as my Savior, I sinned. I made choices that caused hurt to my children and extended family. It is these decisions that are the hardest for me to write about. Pride wants me to sugarcoat them. Fear of acceptance wants me to leave them out altogether—*all the more reason why they must be shared.*

Depending on where you are in your walk with the Lord, some of what I say may not make sense to you but instead will stir a desire in you to learn more. Be open to that process. Jot down any thoughts that are raised or questions that are not answered. Take these to the Lord in prayer. Over time, he will lead you into the answers to those questions. He will not leave you without understanding.

I pray that what I have written will be a blessing to you as you read through these pages. I pray that you will see the deep love I have come to experience from our triune God, and that you too will encounter our Father God; his Son, Jesus; and the Holy Spirit.

—Joyce A. Howard

Joyce A. Howard

My Search for God

As a young child, I wanted to believe in God's existence. On Sunday afternoons I chose to go off by myself to spend time with him. I had a special place outdoors that was warm and sunny and open. It was the roof of our garage, which was large and flat (and a place where I should not have been had my parents known). There, I would hold lengthy debates with God. I would challenge what I had been learning about him through Sunday school and books. (I grew up in the United Methodist Church in a small town in Michigan.) I would question if he really existed, even though I would continue to go there seeking to talk with him. I wanted desperately to know he was real.

Most of all, I would tell God about everything that was

wrong within my family. I would tell him about the drinking and the fighting. I would tell him about other things that happened to me that were very hurtful. There did not seem to be anyone with whom I could discuss these issues. And as a young child, I felt incapable of dealing with them myself. Alone with God, I could let the tears go. I could share with him the hurt, the anguish, and the loneliness I felt. He knew things about me that no one else did.

As I grew and the problems within my life and our family continued, I began to blame God, accusing him of not doing anything about it. I have since discovered that I am really good at placing blame on others, especially on God, and not accepting any personal responsibility for what is wrong.

Salvation and Baptism in the Holy Spirit

On February 26, 1976, I came to a saving knowledge of the Lord Jesus Christ. I was thirty-one years old at the time and had been married for eleven years. Through repentance, Jesus became my personal Savior, and I was filled with his Spirit. This did not happen as a joyous event in the middle of a church service. I met the Lord in my home in the early morning hours through a television evangelist, Pat Robertson, on *The 700 Club*.[2]

At that time I was at a very low point in my life. In fact, I had made the decision to end my life. I was in the process of determining which pills I would take because if I "did it," I wanted to be sure to succeed. I was crying and had the television on to cover my noise. You see, my two children (son, age ten; and daughter, age five) were asleep in their bedrooms. My first husband (we later divorced) was asleep in our bedroom.

In January of 2006, I watched a series of videos by Jack Hayford called *You and Your Angels*.[3] The tapes teach about both the angels of God and fallen angels. On tape two, he talks about how fallen angels try to work in our lives. One of the main things they try to do is whisper fallacy into our minds.

On the video, Pastor Hayford explained about the spirit of suicide. Its goal is to make suicide seem credible, desirable, a positive and wise choice. This spirit leads you to reason that suicide would be the best choice for you and for everyone around you. When I listened to this part of the tape, I realized those were *exactly* my thoughts that night. I was convinced this was the only answer, the best answer for all.

As I sat in front of the television trying to figure out just how to end things, Pat Robertson stopped in the middle of his interview with a guest. He said he felt the Lord telling him to pray right then. He went on to describe me; he said the Lord was showing him a woman sitting in her living room deciding how to end her life. God told him to tell me that suicide was not the answer. He said that God loved me and wanted me to give my life to him. He asked me to kneel down and put my hands on the television screen and pray with him. I did it. At that point I had come to the end of myself, the end of my pride, and I was willing to try anything. He led me in a prayer of salvation, which I repeated in full earnestness to God.

As he led me and I prayed, I felt this heavy weight lift off my body. I knew I had been set free! And I finally knew beyond the shadow of a doubt that the God I had sought and longed to know throughout my childhood was real. He was no longer external; I could feel his presence within me.

Then he prayed for me to be baptized in the Holy Spirit. I began to speak in an unknown language right there in my living room. It just poured forth like a river, and it has never stopped pouring forth to this day.

At the time of my new birth in Christ, I was a smoker, among other bad habits. It was a couple of weeks later when a friend noticed I was not smoking and commented about it to me. I remember looking at her funny and wanting to ask what she was talking about, as I had barely any memory of the fact I had smoked. I never even thought to smoke again. I did not ask to be set free; God just freed me. *It was so far gone as to be forgotten.* Praise God! That is the kind of loving Father we have!

I have reflected many times on the events of that evening (February 26, 1976, when I was born again). One of the things that totally fills my mind with awe is that I was watching a rerun of a show that had played the afternoon before! What Pat Robertson was responding to during that taping was clearly me, and yet, no doubt, others. That is another part of God's miraculous power and grace. It is so beyond my finite mind that I cannot comprehend the magnificence of it.

Charismatic Renewal

I wish I could continue this as you would a fairy tale—how everything was perfect, and I lived happily ever after.

That is not how real life works. There was so much in my life that needed correction. God had not been a part of my life since I had left for college thirteen years earlier. Every attempt I had made to return to church for the sake of my family (husband and children) had failed.

After my rebirth I knew there was one person I could seek out who would understand what had happened to me: my college roommate, Kaye. When I contacted her, she was excited. She invited me to some Christian activities in the area where she lived (Aglow luncheon, Bible study, etc.). I tried doing that but soon realized I would have to find something nearer to where I lived.

The only place closer I knew about was a charismatic prayer group that met in a Catholic church in a neighboring town. Desperate, I went there. Of course, I went in sunglasses and a hat for disguise. I had heard all the stories about the "crazy charismatics" and did not want to be seen among them. After all, I was a teacher and had my reputation to maintain! There were people there who recognized me right away and went out of their way to make me feel welcome. In fact, parents of one of my students were part of the leadership of the group. (Doesn't God have a sense of humor?) I became a regular member and loved it.

My first husband was a lapsed Catholic. I thought this movement toward the Catholic Church would be just the ticket to get his attention. Within no time I had joined the church and helped to form both a Bible study and a prayer group at our local church. People were discovering the personal relationship that God wanted to have with them through his son, Jesus Christ. We were studying the

Bible together, learning to pray for one another's needs, and learning to care for one another. My husband also joined the prayer group.

Under the leading of our pastor, I became the director of our four-parish junior high and high school catechetical center. Besides teaching about the faith, we formed a spirit-filled youth group with an outreach to the area. We held ecumenical youth rallies, again seeing teens commit their lives to the Lord and experience the infilling of the Lord's Spirit. My husband and I became commissioned lay ministers of our diocese.

Does it sound like a fairy tale? If I leave it at just these outward things that others could see, it might seem that way. Unfortunately, there was more, or perhaps I should say there was something lacking. What was lacking was the home life. Nothing changed in the desperate, lonely relationship I shared with my husband. Every attempt on my part to push him more caused an equal and opposite reaction. Each of us makes choices—wise and unwise—in our lives, as in my unwise choice to try to push and manipulate him.

I can tell you exactly when my first marriage ended for me. When the people we were involved with through the lay ministry tricked my husband into agreeing to go on a marriage encounter weekend, I had my fingers crossed. Regardless of how or why he came, I thought God would certainly meet us there and change him. And that is just what seemed to happen. I really believed throughout the weekend that the tears and tenderness shown by my husband were signs of a genuine change of heart. When we left the retreat center and got into our car, I cuddled next to him in the front seat (which I never would have done in the past). I was immediately shoved across the seat, leaving a mark on my arm. He said to me, "If you think that nonsense is continuing in this car or when we get home, you had better think again, because it isn't!" He didn't say another word the whole way home. Instead, he got out his cigarettes and smoked in the car. Up to that point, he had always made a point not to smoke in my presence or in our car or house. That ended that day, as did our marriage for me. I let go of my hope that day. I let go of my belief that God was going to restore my marriage. I gave up on God.

Outwardly, no one knew how miserable I was. I was too proud to admit what was really happening in my life. I did not have the humility I needed to tell the truth. I had grown up in a home where you were taught to "keep the family secrets quiet." In other words, you showed one face to the world, a façade, while a whole other existence took place at home—a philosophy that is based in pride. And I had brought that lie into my marriage.

Pride is such an evil. Pride keeps us from facing the truth. Pride keeps us cornered in our own little world, unable to reach out to others as we should.

So my life continued on in its duality. Eventually I was led to the regional Catholic seminary, where I earned a master's degree in theological studies.[4] Little did I know at the time that this decision would be the one that would turn my world upside down, tearing it in two.

Divorce

Divorce does not happen overnight. It takes years of anguish, tears, unforgiveness, bitterness, unfaithfulness—the many causes, because it is never one—for a divorce to occur. All through those years, choices are made by both parties that lead the couple further apart and closer to divorce.

It was at the seminary that I met the man who would become my second husband. Ted was in his last years of study to be an ordained priest. We met at the seminary during the fall of 1982. By the spring of 1983, we had become friends. We loved biking together, going to movies with friends, bowling in the basement of the seminary, and sharing morning and evening prayer. One of the most precious memories of my life was the day when I prayed with Ted to accept Jesus as his personal Savior. Up to that point in his life, Ted had experienced a great love for God as his father. He believed in the Holy Trinity, but he had never understood that Jesus wanted to have a personal, intimate relationship with him.

It was in June of 1983 that I gave my first husband an ultimatum. I was going to begin counseling. I told him I would give our marriage one more year. He would need to agree to counseling also. If we could not change our relationship during that year, I would make plans to leave. By this time, my son was entering his senior year in high school. He and I talked together. He knew about everything that was happening between his father and me. He knew that I was in counseling. And he knew about Ted.

My first husband chose not to enter counseling. He

Joyce A. Howard

knew that our son was aware of what was happening, but he insisted that we say nothing to our daughter, who was younger. Right or wrong, I agreed to the arrangement.

During the year I was in counseling, Ted and I saw very little of each other, as he was no longer at the seminary. Ted was ordained as a priest during the fall of that year. He was assigned as an associate pastor of a church in the southwestern part of the state. I needed that time to make a decision about my first marriage.

Working with the counselor, I reached the decision to separate. In June of 1984 I graduated from seminary and took a job at a Catholic church in another town. The decision came as a shock to my children and to my family and friends. Except for a very few who were aware of what was happening, they felt blindsided by the move. It was difficult for them to process the speed and magnitude of the change. My son went off to college that fall, and I had shared custody of my daughter. Family members tried to come to terms with the separation. Some people who had been my friends for years were not able to make the transition. Others "fell away" for a season but returned to become a part of my life again.

Despite everything, it was a blessed year. I met some spirit-filled women who were dear sisters in the Lord. Together, we were in charge of catechetical teaching for the children and teens of the church where I was working. As had happened earlier, a spirit-filled youth group formed; we hosted various gatherings and felt a great movement of the Lord among the youth of the church.

After I separated and moved, Ted and I began to see

27

more of each other. He would come up to visit me on his day off. I would travel to where he was to spend time together. Ted's loves of biking, camping, and hiking became shared loves of mine. In March of 1985 I began the process of meeting with a lawyer for divorce. Ted was meeting with his spiritual director and also working with a counselor. Eventually, he made the decision to leave the priesthood.

Marriage to Ted

Ted and I were married on July 26, 1986. For our honeymoon we hiked in the Smoky Mountains. We biked in many parts of the state, plus camped and hiked. Our lives became like two halves of one whole. We were on the road doing something almost every weekend. We were so glad that we did; that made it easier for him to accept his immobility a few years later.

The Battle of MS

Shortly after Ted and I were married, he started to experience the symptoms of MS (multiple sclerosis). At the time, we did not realize that was what was wrong. It took a year for the diagnosis to be confirmed. At that point, no one realized how prevalent MS was going to be within his family. (Over a dozen family members have since been diagnosed.) The symptoms began with numbness and tingling in Ted's arms. Next, vision problems developed. It didn't take long for his gait to be affected to the point that strangers who saw him walking thought that he was drunk.

Within five years of our marriage, Ted could no longer work. He probably should have quit working a year earlier than he did, but he was determined to keep going as long as he could. Ted went from backpacking and bicycling to using a walker within five years. What a shock! We reverberated from the speed of the change!

We were praying people. During this time, we attended a spirit-filled, praying church. We prayed for his healing, as did our church family. Despite it all, heaven seemed to be closed. No healing. No words of knowledge to explain God's plan. Only silence. Well, not only silence—love. We always felt God's love. We never felt forsaken or punished or unloved. But we never found the answer we were seeking—his healing.

At the same time my husband was no longer able to work, I finished my master's degree and began to teach at a community college. Life became a constant run between the demands at the college and my husband's progressive disease. Throughout it all, it was God's love that sustained us. There was never a question about whether we would stick it out. Our love for each other never diminished despite the struggles. In fact, our love for each other was actually strengthened each time we passed through a crisis.

Ted's illness overshadowed our lives in so many ways. It stretched our faith. Dependence on the Lord became a way of life for time, energy, finances, etc. The portion of my husband's medical expenses we paid in 1999 alone totaled over twenty-one thousand dollars. Try to fit that into a budget that is not inspired and blessed by the Lord!

For many years my husband required oxygen and suctioning twenty-four-seven, a hospital bed that could be elevated, use of an enteral feeding pump, and other equipment that required a constant supply of electricity. God's hand of provision was constant; not once in all those years were we without. There were times when the people and businesses two blocks north of us had no power, the people and businesses south and east of us had no power, and yet we had power. This amazed our friends. God cares; he cares about our needs. He will meet you in your needs.

People have asked me how I made it through the struggles of Ted's illness, including all the hospital stays. How did I keep going? I had the Spirit of God in me to turn to and rely on. God's Spirit saw me through twenty-four hospital stays, adding up to over two hundred days, between 1992 and 2005. The Spirit of God kept me going, and he will keep you going too. The bulk of those hospital stays began by ambulance. As I followed the ambulance carrying my husband to the hospital, I prayed the whole way there. Sometimes I prayed in English, but often that was not enough given the stress. This was when my heavenly prayer language meant the most to me. Through praying in the Spirit, I could make contact with God in a way I could not on my own. The Holy Spirit knew better than I did what to pray for.

> Likewise the Spirit also helps in our weaknesses. For we do not know what we should pray for as we ought, but the Spirit Himself makes intercession for us with groanings which cannot be uttered. Now He who searches the hearts knows what the mind of the Spirit *is*, because He makes intercession for the saints according to *the will of* God.
>
> Romans 8:26–27

I do not mean to imply that there were no struggles, no anguish in those times and events. There were! Not long ago I had gotten on to the expressway heading south when a paramedic's vehicle with its lights flashing came up the expressway from the opposite direction. I have seen many ambulances and paramedic vehicles since 2005, but on this day, the memory hit me full force, bringing forth tears to my eyes.

As I drove, I recalled the fear, loneliness, and despair the enemy had tried to use to grab hold of me and dominate me during those trips. I recalled how the Lord enabled me to pray in the Spirit to strengthen my inner man in the midst of the battle. I remembered battling to stay in faith, to believe in the Lord as the fierceness of the storm around me tried to take me under. What a testimony to the faithfulness of the Lord!

As my family and friends will attest, when Ted was in the hospital, I was there too. I spent every night with him; he was never alone. When and if I had to be gone during the day, family and friends came to take up the slack for me.

My estimation of our *personal* portion of Ted's medical expenses during those years of 1992 to 2005 was over

182,000 dollars. That averaged fourteen thousand dollars a year out of our budget (my salary as a teacher) for just obvious medical expenses. That amounted to almost twelve hundred dollars a month for one hundred and fifty-six months nonstop. It shocks me to even write it! And yet the Lord provided.

You may be wondering why I mention the issue of money. Here are three reasons. First, we need to understand the financial struggle people are under when there is a major illness within their family. We need to have compassion toward these families and be willing to help in any way we can. That may mean providing care and support. That may mean assisting with financial burdens.

Second, the spending of that money gave me thirteen more years with Ted. I would spend it all again, and even more, to have him with me. Money's value should be to further personal relationships and God's purposes in our lives. The world tells us money's value is to buy a bigger home, a fancier car, or designer clothes. The world tells us we haven't "made it" unless we have compiled a fortune in savings and bonds and traveled around the world. But Jesus' message regarding money has everything to do with the furtherance of his kingdom and little to do with our worldly image.

Third, I want you to realize that God would never willingly cause such financial hardship for a family. I hope you can see that sickness, disease, and poverty are *not* from the Lord; they are the tactics of Satan. They are the means by which Satan tries to turn us against God. Satan wants us to blame God for the circumstances we are in, for when we blame God, we cut ourselves off from his blessings.

Ted's Last Year

July of 2004 was the beginning of Ted's last year on this earth. Not knowing that, but so absolutely fitting, we had a big party that day to celebrate his life. As preparation for the celebration, Ted's sister, Riky, and I put together a book on his life.

The last part of the book was the place where I wrote about him, beginning with this scripture:

> Love suffers long *and* is kind; love does not envy; love does not parade itself, is not puffed up; does not behave rudely, does not seek its own, is not provoked, thinks no evil; does not rejoice in iniquity, but rejoices in the truth; bears all things, believes all things, hopes all things, endures all things. And now abide faith, hope, love, these three; but the greatest of these *is* love.
>
> 1 Corinthians 13:4–7, 13

I wrote the following about Ted:

For me, this scripture is a description of my husband. You could easily substitute his name for "love" and it would read the same. I also realize it is a description of Jesus. It was this built-in love that allowed Jesus to pass through his agony and crucifixion. And it is this built-in love that allows my husband to pass through the agony and crucifixion of his illness. When I see how he handles his illness, I understand how Jesus was able to endure.

Ted does not get angry. He does not strike out at others. He is not into self-pity, and he does not display a woe-is-me attitude. It is not blind acceptance, like he is just giving up, but acceptance in Christ for what is asked of him. And all the time, he is expressing love to those around him by his patience and kindness.

Ted doesn't question or blame God. He is not jealous or envious of the good health others have. Many patients with extended illnesses become bitter and hard, not him. Even when I lose my patience and am feeling the pressure of the demands of his care, he understands and forgives and keeps no record of wrongs.[5]

Ted was such an example of faith. He faced the struggle of his illness with complete trust in the Lord. Jesus was not only his guide in health but also the person on whom Ted anchored his life, even in the battle of MS.

But Kaye

Ted was in the hospital twice during January of 2005, totaling to eighteen days. After the second stay he was sent home with untreatable, drug-resistant urinary tract and bloodstream infections. The doctors told us there was nothing more that could be done for him and that we needed to make other decisions. Hospice started on February 23, 2005. My sister, Deb, went with me to the funeral home on the third of March to begin making preparations. Ted's longtime friend Bob came from out of state to see him on the tenth of March to say his good-byes. Our niece Anna and her husband, Roman, also came to see Ted. Others came too, believing these would be their last times to see Ted alive.

But Kaye, my roommate from college, didn't see it that way. She and her husband, Rich, had come to the hospital to pray with Ted. After that visit she started e-mailing each week, saying that they were praying and that the Lord had told them he wanted to heal Ted. With her help we made the decision to seriously pray again for Ted to be healed. Kaye came on the thirtieth of March, and we did just that. She brought us a series of healing scriptures we were to pray each day, plus cassette tapes, books, and videos that dealt with healing. Here we were praying for his total healing in the midst of hospice. It seemed crazy!

Amazingly, he started getting better right away. It was not long before he went from lying in bed almost comatose to wanting to be up, dressed, and in his recliner. Next, he wanted to be in his wheelchair and outside with me. At

Called to Be Different

first we kept him hooked up to his oxygen, but we soon discovered he didn't need it anymore, verified with a pulse oximeter we carried with us.

We noticed that his arms, which had been totally stiff and heavy like dead weights, were losing their stiffness and becoming movable. He could not *will* them to move, but I could pick them up and move them without contractions. His doctor agreed that what he was experiencing was a miracle. He reinstated his therapies and sent him to a neurological specialist.

In May we arranged for Kaye's pastor to come to our house to pray with Ted, along with the youth pastor and another of the church elders (plus Kaye, who is also an elder in their church). We had a great time sharing, praying, and praising the Lord. He was blessed by the prayers, filled with the Spirit, and experienced further healing. We made the decision not to continue hospice, which ended on May 23, 2005, exactly three months from when it began.

After the gathering with Kaye's church leaders, Ted asked that we go to Kaye's church the next Sunday. At the church service, the pastor had me bring Ted to the front. He asked everyone to lay hands on, or stretch their hands toward, my husband while he prayed and anointed him with oil. It was a tremendous experience. We were able to go back to the church for several Sundays. We loved singing and praising the Lord. We were blessed by everyone there.

Ted's Last Week

During what turned out to be the last week of his life, we met with many of Ted's specialists. The neurological specialist was trying my husband on some new medications that would help with his neuromuscular control and felt confident he would make improvement. The occupational therapist (OT) was very pleased with how well his arms had improved, with full rotation at his shoulders, elbows, and wrists, and full finger movement possible.

The physical therapist was amazed at how far and fast his legs were straightening. During her visit, she came out to the living room pumping her arms and saying, "You have to come and see! I just got his hips to the standing position!" We talked about how it had taken four to six weeks for his arms to become movable again, and we seemed to be on the same timetable for his legs. We were all very excited, including Ted. Wc were full of hope that he would continue to regain his ability to function and control his own body and life.

I will never forget what happened in one of those last visits. The OT was trying to help us determine how Ted could operate a motorized wheelchair and a computer. As the OT was discussing all the possibilities, he said, "If only he could smack his lips and—" As quickly as he said those words, before he could even complete the sentence, Ted smacked his lips so loud that I am sure the neighbors could have heard him. It was as if he was telling us, "Look, I am still in here, in this body; I can do more than you believe I can." The OT was astounded. He asked him to repeat the action, which my husband did. He apologized to him and told him he was sorry for not believing he could do that and just assuming he could not when he had never asked him to try.

Oh my! How often do we do that to others? How ready are we to *not* believe (i.e. act on unbelief) without checking with the Spirit of God? We do this without thinking to people who are ill, and we do this without thinking to people who are well. *Unbelief is an insidious act we must become aware of.*

Often, when we think of belief and unbelief, we think of it only in the context of our relationship with God (and, of course, it is essential that we do have belief in God). What we are unaware of is the unbelief we are expressing toward other people and toward circumstances that occur in our everyday life. In point of fact, *that is exactly where the Lord wants us to display our belief in him—through our situations, circumstances, and relationships with others.*

Part of our daily prayer must be to ask the Lord to open our eyes to situations in our lives where we are expressing unbelief. We must pray as Jesus taught his disciples, "Do not lead us into temptation, but deliver us from the evil one" (Matthew 6:13). We must pray that the Lord will gently reveal to us all the ways and times that we are walking in doubt and unbelief. We must pray to be set free.

Repentance

So much happened in those last four months of Ted's life here on earth. What made the difference after all those years of praying? The Lord revealed many things to us that had blocked Ted's healing. In March of that year, my husband and I discovered we were on the wrong road, going in the wrong direction. We discovered that God was no longer first in our lives and first in our marriage. We discovered there was *much* we needed to repent for, especially me.

Unlike Ted, there was bitterness and resentment in me for things that had happened over the years. I had to "get right with God" about all those things. I had to confess sins that had been present in my life, issues I had been refusing to own up to. I had to forgive wrongs that were done to me, even by my closest family and friends. Surprisingly, what I discovered is this: *the closer the person is to you, the more chance there is for unforgiven hurts and wrongs to exist.* When we repent, we change our minds about the things we have been allowing to drag us down and away from the Lord.

I never really understood repentance until I heard

41

Called to Be Different

Kenneth Copeland share about a dream he had.[6] In the dream, he had been in Dallas, Texas, and was trying to go to Austin. Now, to get from Dallas to Austin, you would take I-35 south. But he was on I-35 north, which leads to Oklahoma City, Oklahoma. He said he saw himself praying and crying out to the Lord, asking God to help him to reach Austin on time. He said he watched himself cry, plead, pray, and do everything he could to get God to help him to reach Austin. But the whole time he kept seeing road signs showing him that he was going north and getting closer to Oklahoma City.

Finally, in desperation he cried out to the Lord and said, "Lord, what am I doing wrong? Why can't I get to Austin where I want to go?" The Lord answered him, "Son, I hear you. I hear all your prayers and see your tears. I have been waiting for you to ask me what was wrong and why your prayers were not being answered. Son, turn around! You are going in the wrong direction!" Immediately he realized God was talking to him about repentance.

How many of us are going in the wrong direction? How many of us are crying out to God, but our prayers are going unanswered? "God, I go to church every Sunday. I pray every day. I try to help others. Why are you not hearing me?"

How many of us need to repent? Do you? If so, it is okay to stop right now and allow the Lord to reveal to you issues of sin in your life. Confess them and receive forgiveness. It will bring you such a world of peace.

The Lord's Preparation

During June of 2005 Ted and I began praying in earnest to the Lord about what his call was for the two of us. As we both had ministry backgrounds, and as his health continued to improve, we were sure God would lead us into full-time ministry together. We didn't know where or how, but it seemed to be what would happen.

Just two days before his departure, Ted and I were watching Billy Joe and Sharon Daugherty's *Victory in Jesus* program on television.[7] He was really enjoying the sermon, so I asked him if he wanted me to see if it could be ordered from their Web site. So off I went to victory. com, a Web site I had never visited before.[8] Little did I know what I was going to find. It was then I discovered they had their own accredited Bible college called VBI or Victory Bible Institute.[9]

When I clicked on the VBI off-campus link, here is what it said: "If you can't come to VBI, VBI will come to you." I had come in to the computer to find a video for my husband, and instead it seemed I was finding the answer to our prayers. Here we had just talked and prayed together if the Lord might be calling us into ministry and had questioned how we could get ready for such a thing from our home, and I was perhaps looking at the answer to that prayer. And here we were in the midst of setting goals for my husband to be able to use a computer sometime over the next year.

Ted was sitting in his recliner in the living room watching a Christian program on the television. I went out to him and started telling him about everything I had come across on victory.com. After I told him about the online part, he agreed this might be an answer to our prayer. I said, "Let's pray right now!" I knelt down next to him in his chair, and we joined hands, interlocking arms, and prayed. I thanked the Lord for what I had found on the computer, and we prayed that God would let us know if this was what he might have in mind for us. We talked about the fact that neither of us was obviously ready to start such a thing, but maybe we would be by the next summer. Hopefully by then Ted would be able to operate a computer and a motorized wheelchair. We would have the whole year to pray and work out the plans, all the while with him improving physically.

Since our anniversary was in ten days, I said, "Let's pray right now and recommit ourselves to each other." So we did. We pledged our continued love for each other and to our marriage and recommitted our marriage to God. I asked Ted to forgive me for any wrongs I had done against him, anytime I had been short or selfish or unwilling to help him. He let me know that he forgave me and then asked to do the same toward me. I told him I doubted there was anything to be forgiven but that I forgave him also.

It was then I realized (the Lord revealed to me) that I needed to forgive the MS. I told Ted I forgave him for having MS and all the hardships that the MS had brought to our marriage. It was not his fault he had MS, but I realized that *in my heart I was holding the effects of the MS against Ted.*

Next, I forgave God for allowing, not causing, the MS to be in Ted, and I forgave God for allowing, not causing, MS to be in his family. It was really Satan who had caused the MS, not God, but I realized that *in my heart I was holding the effects of the MS against God*, just as I was holding them against Ted. I asked God's forgiveness for this distorted view and for blaming him for the effects of sin in my life. Ted wanted to do the same. He forgave God for allowing, not causing, the MS to be in him, and he forgave God for allowing, not causing, MS to be in his family. He asked God's forgiveness for blaming those effects of sin on him.

I then realized that I needed to ask God's forgiveness for my divorce. I asked God to forgive me for giving up on my first marriage. I asked God to forgive me for the hurt and anguish this had caused to my children, my first husband, and our families and friends. You see, it does not matter what all the causes of the divorce were; what God wanted of me was that I own my part in the cause. I then prayed and asked God to heal the effects of that sin (the divorce) upon myself, Ted, my first husband, my children, our families, and our friends, the many consequences of that sin.

Next, I realized that I needed to ask God's forgiveness for my decision to remarry. I asked his forgiveness for the hurt and anguish that decision had caused to my children and to my family and friends. I had to acknowledge to the Lord how my actions had affected the others in my life. It was not easy for them to make the transition to this new person I was choosing to devote my life to, and I needed to ask God's forgiveness for putting that additional burden upon them.

Ted then let me know he wanted to ask forgiveness for his decisions. He asked God to forgive his decision to leave the priesthood and marry. Not that God was against our marriage; he was not, but Ted had walked away from a commitment he had made to the church and to the people of the church. He wanted God to forgive him for those choices but, more importantly, to forgive the hurt and anguish those choices had brought to his family, friends, church members, and fellow priests.

After we were through with this, I asked that we pray together again for his healing. I prayed, "Lord, we ask for total healing, body, soul and spirit, from the top of his head to the soles of his feet." We often prayed this way for Ted, so that was not new, but the context in which it was happening was certainly new. We sealed it with "I love you" and with hugs and kisses and then got him ready for bed. Neither of us was aware of what would take place less than two days later.

Ted's Last Day on Earth

On the day Ted died (July 17, 2005) he had a slight fever, and we had no plans till later in the day. We got him up and into the shower. Our tradition for shower time was to put on a Christian CD, something really lively, at seventy-three decibels. Yes, loud! I would sing and dance around to the music for the two of us. So that is what we did. I had *The Best of the Gaither Vocal Band*[10], disc one, playing. After I finished washing him, I asked if he wanted to stay a little longer. He nodded that he did. So I propped the handheld showerhead so that it would run on his back.

"A Brand New Song" was playing at the time, which is

a song about going to heaven. I danced and sang my way into the bedroom. I made the bed to "He Touched Me" then danced and sang my way back into the bathroom to "Good, Good News." I had a towel sitting on the counter and picked it up on my way by. I started to dry him off and was talking and singing away when I realized he was not responding. I stopped and said his name. He did not respond. I said his name again and asked if he was sleeping. No response. Part of me knew right then he was gone.

These are the words to the song "A Brand New Song," the song that was playing when I left the bathroom: [11]

> Today could be the day when Jesus calls me away, up high above the sky, where I will live and never die. So don't weep for me when I cross over that sea. My pain will all be gone and I will have a brand new song to sing. Imagine a home where fear and doubt are never known. No more, for all is peace. Sounds like the perfect place to me. If you get there first, I'll join you on the second verse. And for eternity, you and I will have a brand new song to sing. Today could be the day.

And it was! I believe an angel came down to him. He whispered, "Shush" and took my husband's hands, and they flew off together. He just left! I am so thankful there was *no* struggle for him. No gasping for a last breath, no fighting and becoming delirious, nothing. God just allowed him to peacefully leave his earthly body and take his rightful place in heaven. And I believe he was singing and dancing and cheering as he went. I am certain that as I was singing "Good, Good News" here on earth to his earthly body, he was singing "Good, Good News" to Jesus in his new spiritual body. What a way to go; he simply went from glory to glory!

I am so thankful to the Lord that Ted's death was not associated with an emergency ambulance run or a stay in the hospital. He allowed Ted to leave this earth right from the peace and comfort of our home. He allowed Ted to leave in the midst of our worship and praise of him. What a blessing! What favor! I am so thankful for the Lord's goodness. I am so thankful for the Lord's ever-enduring and ever-forgiving mercy and grace.

Ted's vigil service was held on July 20, with his funeral on July 21. At the vigil, I shared my experience of being his wife. I shared that I could not recall my husband ever being angry, raising his voice in an abusive manner, or speaking a negative word about another person, including me. It is amazing to think that I could know a man for over twenty-three years and have *no* recollection of him being insulting, snide, angry, gossiping about others, or showing jealousy or envy toward others. *I was his wife for nineteen years and could say that!*

The Bible says we are to be filled with the Spirit, live by the Spirit, and walk by the Spirit. I told everyone at the service that as I had reflected on my marriage, I could honestly say that I felt like I had lived with Jesus for those nineteen years. His whole life exemplified Jesus.

Continuing On

As you can see, it has been impossible for me to tell you about those twenty-three years of my life without discussing Ted. During those years, I did not have a separate life; my life was joined to my husband as one, as Jesus spoke of marriage. I have said many times to people that I would not change those years with my husband for anything. Yes, we had trials. Yes, we were tested. But the Lord was there through it all, blessing and protecting, and most of all, sharing his love with us. I miss my husband, yet I am fully at peace with the fact that he is alive and fulfilled in heaven. Yes, his earthly body is dead and buried, but his spirit is with Jesus. The part of us that was made to be eternal is *eternally existing* with the great Creator.

These words of Paul the Apostle are recorded for us in Philippians: "For to me, to live *is* Christ, and

Called to Be Different

49

to die *is* gain. For I am hard-pressed between the two, having a desire to depart and be with Christ, *which is* far better" (Philippians 1:21, 23).

The Lord has given me a spirit of joy. Yes, I grieve Ted's loss, but I do not dwell on those negatives. I refuse to give place in my being to a spirit of grief. I dwell on the goodness of the Lord. I dwell on the fact that our destiny is heaven, and my husband has achieved that. This was the question for me, "Where will your focus be: on death or on eternal life?" I choose life! I look to the Lord to meet my needs as a widow, for his Word says, "The LORD watches over the strangers; He relieves the fatherless and widow; But the way of the wicked He turns upside down" (Psalm 146:9).

Ted will always be a part of who I am, but the Lord is not finished with me yet. For the most part, I believe I have tried to seek his direction for my life and have followed him. His words for me have been *redirection* and *regeneration*.

In April of 2006 I chose to take part in water baptism by immersion to let my family and friends and, in particular, the Lord Jesus know that I was committing my life to him.[12] For me, water baptism was the sign that I was choosing to die to my selfish desires and instead choosing to be Christ's follower. I was allowing my old self that had been enslaved to sin to be buried in the waters of baptism so that I was resurrected into new life, freed from the dominion and bondage of sin. I was following Jesus' example of water baptism so that I too could be filled to overflowing with the gift of the Holy Spirit.

"For as many of you as were baptized into Christ have

put on Christ" (Galatians 3:27). This is my hope: that I have *put on* Christ's nature and *become* Christ to those around me in my family, neighborhood, and on the job.

Do you believe that the Lord Jesus loves you, cares about you, and wants to use you through the actions of your everyday life to reach others? So many people come to church "going through the motions" but do not really believe that God wants to use them. *Your everyday life is your mission field.* We are called to be witnesses and missionaries of the Lord. We are called to be apostles, prophets, and evangelists in the workplace, in our neighborhoods, and in our homes.

These have been God's questions to me. Are your children and grandchildren walking with the Lord? Are your friends walking with the Lord? Are your neighbors walking with the Lord?

He has called me to make major changes in where and how I spend my time and money, the focus of "things" in my home, and how my life and home are organized. He has helped me to change what I value, things I never thought about before. He has caused me to look at my attitudes, my actions, and my language.

I pray now to seek the Lord's direction on what to spend my money on, as I realize it is a gift from the Lord, and it is meant to be used to further his kingdom here on earth. As he directs, I give to individuals, Christian charities, and of course, to my church. More and more, my thoughts and attitudes are focused on what is eternal. I am trying to bring my actions into agreement with that, and I hope my language matches, that it expresses

Called to Be Different

the hope and love and joy of our Father in whom we live and dwell and have our being.

This is what the Lord has been dealing with me about since my husband moved on to heaven. I am called to be different. *We are called to be different.* Different in how we live our everyday lives and relate to the people around us, by the choices we make about how we use our time and money, by the things we expose our eyes and ears and minds to, by how we grieve the loss of a loved one, and by how we view our retirement years. In short, by all the actions of our lives. We are called *out* of the world, not to behave and react as the rest of the world does.

Yes, life goes on around us. *But what matters is what we will take into eternity with us.* It is not about having the biggest house, best flowerbeds, biggest garden, the best job or car or clothes. It is not about winning awards and accolades here on earth. It is not about the best anything as judged by earthly standards.

There are still areas in my life that need healing and wholeness. In January of 2006 I watched a series of videos called *The Landmines of the Believer.*[13] The first video was on pride. I had to watch that three or four times before the Spirit of God freed me to move on. (No doubt I will be directed to watch it again.) Pride was Lucifer's sin. Pride causes self-centeredness. It covers up feelings of insufficiency and inadequacy. Pride between me and the Lord means I am not being honest with him and looking to him as my source.

God shows us our sin because he loves us. He knows the harm that sin does to us. Sin is part of the curse that came into the world when Adam and Eve disobeyed God.

Kenneth Copeland says that *sin is a blessing blocker*.[14] I like that description. Sin separates us from God, who is the source of all blessing in our lives.

As I turn my life over more and more to the lordship of Christ Jesus, sin must leave. One cannot happen without the other. Jesus is so patient. He is so gentle. He does not condemn. He does not say, "I told you so." Sometimes I hear parents say that over and over again to their children who have gone astray; it becomes a mantra for them. And what does it achieve but condemnation, guilt, and depression? It has the exact opposite effect of what Jesus' loving acceptance does. When Jesus reveals sin to me, he shows it to me in the context of his love. He shows me not just the sin, but the why and the how of it. He helps me to let go of it, to repent, to turn around. He sets me free!

This is what Jesus helped both Ted and me to do on July fifteenth, two nights before Ted's heavenly homecoming. Jesus allowed me to do this on January 26, 1976, when I first repented and asked him into my life. He has allowed me to do this at other points in my walk with him since 1976, and I know he will continue to guide me and help me.

"Love does not rejoice in iniquity, but rejoices in the truth" (1 Corinthians 13:6). Jesus never rejoices in the effects of sin (iniquity) in people's lives, but he rejoices when truth is revealed and brought about. In the ninth chapter of John, a story is recorded of Jesus passing by a man born blind. His disciples wanted to know whose sin caused the blindness. Jesus' focus was not on the cause or causes; his focus was on the truth of healing and life (in this case sight) being restored to this man.

Jesus is ever interceding for us (Hebrews 7:25). Jesus wants each of us to walk free from sin and its effects (iniquity) in our lives. He wants this for me, and he wants it for you. Jesus reveals sin to me through the Holy Spirit. Scripture says that the Spirit will lead us into all truth, and he does. Jesus and the Spirit are waiting for us to call out to them. They waited for me to call out to them. They are waiting for you to do the same.

Earlier I shared this as part of Kenneth Copeland's story on repentance. The Lord answered him, "Son, I hear you. I hear all your prayers and see your tears. I have been waiting for you to ask me what was wrong and why your prayers were not being answered. Son, turn around! You are going the wrong direction!"[15]

I now understand that when God does not answer my prayer, especially over a period of time, there is most likely sin involved. Sin blocks the Lord's ability to answer my prayer. This is such an important lesson. I pray that I will remember it, that I will allow the Holy Spirit to remind me of it. My hope is that I will reach a point in my walk with the Lord that I will look for unconfessed sin in my life before I pray. *Repentance is a lifelong decision, one that needs to be carried out every day.*

My sisters and I were led by the Lord to begin a Bible study together in May of 2005. How intuitive of the Lord to know that I would need that comfort and support just two months later when Ted passed on to heaven. What a blessing our time together was. The Lord helped us to share issues from our childhood that we had never discussed. He showed us blessings that had been within our family throughout the generations. He brought so much healing to us. He called us to intercessory prayer on behalf of our extended families so that no one would be left behind.

Ask yourself this: who among your families do you *not* want to be with you in heaven? For us, we wanted everyone to be there. And that is how the Lord directed us to pray—to bring every name before him, speak it out, decree, and claim them for the Lord. We were not to allow any form of hurt or unbelief to cloud our prayer.

In April of 2007 our family held the first in a series of women-only family Bible studies. This included my sister and some of her daughters and daughters-in-law. We were truly blessed and healed as a family through these gatherings. Not everyone was able to come, but those who could were definitely blessed. We prayed as a family over each woman, laying hands on her and anointing her with oil. Truly, the kingdom of God is coming to our family and flowing out through us to friends, neighbors, co-workers, etc. We are truly blessed!

My Journey of Faith

Abraham went out in faith in his search to follow the Lord. I must do this also. I must hear the call of the Lord Jesus Christ:

> And Jesus came and spoke to them, saying, "All authority has been given to Me in heaven and on earth. Go therefore and make disciples of all the nations, baptizing them in the name of the Father and of the Son and of the Holy Spirit, teaching

them to observe all things that I have commanded you; and lo, I am with you always, *even* to the end of the age." Amen.

Matthew 28:18–20

I have led small fellowship groups that have met in my home. I have been a volunteer chaplain at the county jail. My day job has been as an associate professor at a community college, teaching the healthcare students. I am enrolled in an off-campus ministry training program. What the Lord has in mind for the future, I do not know. I do know that my life is changing and that the Lord is leading me.

When Ted went to be with the Lord right in the midst of his healing, people questioned me as to why that happened. Of course I had no answers except that my trust was in the Lord. There was a definite peace, the Lord telling me that it was okay. There were many signs that showed me that the Lord had it all in his hands. I am comforted knowing I will find out why when I get to heaven.

The best thing that ever happened in my life was finding Jesus. Accepting him as my Savior and Lord has totally changed my life. This did not become a reality in one moment or one day. It has taken me since February of 1976 to turn my life over to Jesus. And it is a process that will not end, God willing, until the day I move on to eternity.

We must get ourselves ready to meet the Lord. Whether our destiny in God is to meet him individually at the time of our death or to meet him at the time of his glorious return, we must be ready. Think about this: every one of us will live for eternity. That is our destiny! The only question is, will we choose an eternity *with* the Lord in heaven or an eternity *without* him in hell? We can try to ignore the question, deny the question, or refuse to answer the question. We can try any tactic we want. However, it will not change the outcome. Dying is something that is going to happen, resulting in our going to one of those two destinations.

There are several aspects to what the Lord has shown me concerning what it means to be "called to be different." In the chapters that follow, I will share the areas of my life that the Lord has changed ... or, more appropriately, continues to change. We must get ourselves ready to serve the Lord while we are still here on earth. We must seek his desire for our lives. We must see the value of our everyday lives, how God desires to work through us to reach others.

Intimacy

Intimacy is one of the areas in our lives where we are called to be different. It was one of the first areas where the Lord began to teach me and lead me. Each of us is born with an internal desire for intimacy. One of the main ways our society tells us to fill that need is through sexual relationships. What I learned is that this built-in need can only truly be filled through Jesus.

I want to share an experience I had when the Lord made himself known to me. It was a moment in which I needed great comfort and assurance. It was the day we celebrated my husband's departure from this earth (July 21, 2005). Our culture refers to these celebrations as funerals. I prefer to call it Ted's homecoming celebration, as eternity is our real home.

After the service and luncheon at the church, family and friends came over to our house. One of my husband's cousins also suffers from MS. Ted and I had decided ahead of time that if anything should happen to him, I was to pass on his equipment, supplies, etc., to our cousin, including our handicap-accessible van. One of our goals that day was to disassemble and pack up the supplies (hospital bed, Hoyer lift, various adaptive devices, etc.). It took all of the van space plus a pickup truck to transport it.

As the afternoon and evening wore on, people slowly began to leave, many having to make the journey to other parts of the state. Finally, everyone was gone and there was just me. Because I had not lived alone for any great length of time, the silence was deafening. I cleaned up what was left to do and then spent a little time in meditation, reading from the Bible. However, I was exhausted and unable to concentrate. I decided I needed to call it a day. I got ready, turned out the lights, and made my way into bed.

As soon as I laid my head on the pillow, a marvelous glow of light entered the room. It literally flowed back and forth over the length of the bed and throughout the room. With it came a weighty presence. It felt as if I was being wrapped up, like a mother would wrap a baby in swaddling clothes. It was the most comforting sensation I can remember. It was a weight that did not press but filled the very air with comfort and peace.

I knew this was the Lord, a manifestation of his presence to comfort me. I spoke to him and thanked him. I knew I was safe and would *never* be alone. I knew he was there and would continue to be there throughout the remainder of my life here on earth. I was able to let go and fall asleep. It meant so much to me that the Lord would reveal his presence to me in this most intimate way at that moment. He knew I was at my very weakest, and he knew how much I needed to experience the assurance of his presence. In that moment, he confirmed his love for me. I knew I could trust him beyond the shadow of a doubt to be my comforter and my protector.

Intimacy is defined as a close, personal relationship, having a detailed knowledge of another resulting from a close or long association or study.[16] Jesus had this with his Father, our Father. Whenever he could, he went off alone to a quiet place to pray. He began and ended his day with his Father. He spent time in prayer and meditation on God's Word. Repeatedly, Jesus said that he only did what he saw his Father doing and only said what he heard his Father saying.

We have Jesus in our hearts (our spirits) through repentance and the baptism of the Holy Spirit. Jesus and the Father dwell in us. There is nothing more intimate than that! The power of the Holy Spirit flows through us. But we have a choice. We can acknowledge the Lord's presence and allow him to speak to us and guide us by his Spirit, or we can stubbornly ignore the promptings of the Spirit. We can accept the love flowing through us and share it with others, or we can allow our hearts to become callous and hardened. As Jesus did, we can spend time in prayer and meditation, so that we can say as Jesus said that we only do and say what we hear Jesus and the Father doing and saying through the Spirit.

When I Carried You

When I first met Ted, we were simply acquaintances. We attended the same seminary and were in many of the same classes. I knew him as a student who studied the Bible and had a deep faith. As time went by, a group of students began to spend time together outside of classes. Both of us were part of that group. We went to movies, bowling, and out to eat, the typical things that groups of friends do.

Then we reached a point where we began to prefer to be alone together. We enjoyed talking about the Lord, praying together, going for walks and bike rides, and sitting quietly by the water's edge, listening to the sounds of nature around us. As we did this more and more, sharing both present life experiences and stories from our past, we became friends.

Time was needed to nurture that friendship. The point came when we both recognized we loved each other even beyond the bounds of normal friendship when we made the choice to commit our lives to each other.

And yet, having said all of that, I have not shared when true intimacy occurred for Ted and me. It was not in the joyous times. It was not in the times of sexual union, although those were certainly most intimate. The times when we experienced true intimacy were in the hard times, times when I had to physically care for him during his prolonged illness. It was the times of showering and dressing him, the times of cleaning his colostomy or changing wound dressings. It was the times when it was only he and I, when my strength and faith had to carry both of us.

Perhaps you have read the poem called "Footprints in

Joyce A. Howard

the Sand" by Mary Stevenson.[17] The line that describes intimacy for me is this: "The Lord replied, 'The times when you have seen only one set of footprints in the sand, is when I carried you.'" Jesus has carried me through many points in my life when I was too weak to carry myself. For me, those have been the moments of true intimacy.

The Mind of Christ

Another aspect of intimacy has to do with our minds. The Apostle Paul wrote this to the church in Philippi:

> Finally, brethren, whatever things are true, whatever things *are* noble, whatever things *are* just, whatever things *are* pure, whatever things *are* lovely, whatever things *are* of good report, if *there is* any virtue and if *there is* anything praiseworthy— meditate on these things. The things which you learned and received and heard and saw in me, these do, and the God of peace will be with you.
>
> Philippians 4:8–9

Paul had this level of intimacy with the Lord. He had such intimacy that he could actually exhort the believers in Philippi and all believers (including you and me) to do those things that they saw and heard him doing. Imagine! To be that much in step with the Spirit of the Lord!

Ted and I were blessed to be "of one mind." We saw things the same way. We understood what each other was thinking and feeling. As his illness progressed and he became less able to speak up for himself, I was so easily

Called to Be Different

able to speak for him. Often friends or family or workers would ask him if what I had shared was what he meant. And almost without exception, he would nod his head yes. It was uncanny how Ted could just turn his head and look at me and immediately I would know what it was he wanted to say or if he needed something done. Isn't that a true blessing? That is favor from the Lord.

My desire is to have this same level of intimacy with the Lord Jesus. This is his desire for me also. I want to be able to know what he is thinking. I want to be able to know what he wants and needs of me. I want to be so in tune with his Spirit that he can simply think the thought and I will be able to respond. That will be true favor with the Lord. It may take a lifetime but is a level of intimacy worth the pursuit. I am called to a different kind of intimacy from what the world suggests. I am called to the true intimacy for which I was created. You, too, are called to this intimacy.

The Effects of Sin

A major part of God's call to me to be different has dealt with correcting the effects of sin in my life. Amazingly, I discovered that I had very little true understanding of what God viewed as sin.

I shared earlier that God shows us our sin because he loves us. Sin is a blessing blocker. Sin separates us from God. Christians are prime targets for demonic strongholds. The opening is sin, either personal or generational. Chuck Pierce says:

> Sin which is not dealt with gives Satan a legal right into a situation, even in the life of a believer. Sin gives the enemy a foothold; a secure position that provides a base for further progress or advance-

ment. The blood that Jesus shed on the cross is what we can appropriate to remit or atone for sin, but we must apply it in order for the sin to be remitted. Until repentance has occurred and the blood of Jesus is applied, the sin—and thus Satan's legal right to a foothold—remains intact.[18]

Sin affects the generations. What always got the Israelites in trouble was when they turned from the true and living God to put their faith into other gods, systems, organizations, etc. God views all such involvements as idolatry and witchcraft.

The Lord finds many ways to communicate his truths to me. One of those ways was the movie *One Night with the King*.[19] I wholly recommend it to you. The movie is based on a book by Tommy Tenney, and his book is based on the Old Testament book of Esther.[20] The movie begins by telling how the situation in Esther's day originally came about, which was through a five-hundred-year-old sin. It was through the disobedience of Saul when Samuel told him to destroy a people on God's command, a people who performed child sacrifices. Talk about generational sin. Oh my, I saw it for all it was worth!

When my ancestors got involved in the Masonic and Eastern Star organizations, they sinned. Their sin brought a lack of blessing, a curse, upon our family. This curse will remain in our family and pass through the generations as a weakness or lack of blessing until it is remitted.

The Masons and Eastern Star require secret pledges, use of other rituals, and offer special recognition and favor among their members (one business person to another).

God is opposed to these things. My parents actually got involved through the Methodist Church. My parents got involved because their parents were involved. This has been in our family for at least three, maybe more, generations (I suspect at least ten).

You may have family members who have been part of organizations such as the Masons, or you may be active in such organizations. I understand how this involvement is something that is shared within families through the generations and how involvement is linked with some of the mainstream denominational churches. Each of you will have to seek the Lord about such involvements. There are many books and teachings readily available in the body of Christ that can help you to learn more. I do not write to condemn you but to share what the Lord has revealed to me.

I hold the belief that God created this universe and that there is one true and living God—Father, Son, and Holy Spirit, three in one. From the book of Genesis, we know that God created this world to be without sin. We know that Eve was deceived by the serpent (Satan), and Adam joined her in the sin. Because of their sin, lack of blessing (curse) entered the human race; women have pain in childbirth, there are relational difficulties, people struggle to earn a living, sickness and disease exist, and so many more evils I could not begin to list them.

God did not create man and woman to sin; God created them to fellowship with him. God did not create sickness and disease. We know this because when God became flesh as Jesus, the Son of God, he went around everywhere healing all those who were sick and infirm.

Called to Be Different

67

Jesus healed, delivered, and in every possible way he could, restored everyone he met.

> When evening had come, they brought to Him many who were demon-possessed. And He cast out the spirits with a word, and healed all who were sick, that it might be fulfilled which was spoken by Isaiah the prophet, saying: *"He Himself took our infirmities And bore our sicknesses."*
>
> Matthew 8:16–17

The Blessing or the Curse

In various places in Scripture, God lays out a choice for us between a blessing and a curse. Here are two of them.

> Behold, I set before you today a blessing and a curse: the blessing, if you obey the commandments of the LORD your God which I command you today; and the curse, if you do not obey the commandments of the LORD your God, but turn aside from the way which I command you today, to go after other gods which you have not known.
>
> Deuteronomy 11:26–28

> See, I have set before you today life and good, death and evil, in that I command you today to love the LORD your God, to walk in His ways, and to keep His commandments, His statutes, and His judgments, that you may live and multiply; and the LORD your God will bless you in the land which you go to possess.
>
> Deuteronomy 30:15–16

Joyce A. Howard

Our Father's desire is to bless us. He wants each of us to walk in the fullness of his blessings. He asks us to make the choice—to choose life, to choose his blessing. *This is an actual choice we have to make.* We first make it when we give our hearts to the Lord through repentance, asking God to become our Savior and Lord. This is a choice we continue to make after salvation; we choose to walk with the Lord, follow his ways, and be led by his Spirit.

The first fourteen verses of Deuteronomy list the blessings that God wants us to walk in:

> Now it shall come to pass, if you diligently obey the voice of the LORD your God, to observe carefully all His commandments which I command you today, that the LORD your God will set you high above all nations of the earth. And all these blessings shall come upon you and overtake you, because you obey the voice of the LORD your God:
>
> Blessed *shall* you *be* in the city, and blessed *shall* you *be* in the country.
>
> Blessed *shall be* the fruit of your body, the produce of your ground and the increase of your herds, the increase of your cattle and the offspring of your flocks.
>
> Blessed *shall be* your basket and your kneading bowl.
>
> Blessed *shall* you *be* when you come in, and blessed *shall* you *be* when you go out.
>
> The LORD will cause your enemies who rise against you to be defeated before your face; they shall come out against you one way and flee before you seven ways.

The LORD will command the blessing on you in your storehouses and in all to which you set your hand, and He will bless you in the land which the LORD your God is giving you.

The LORD will establish you as a holy people to Himself, just as He has sworn to you, if you keep the commandments of the LORD your God and walk in His ways. Then all peoples of the earth shall see that you are called by the name of the LORD, and they shall be afraid of you. And the LORD will grant you plenty of goods, in the fruit of your body, in the increase of your livestock, and in the produce of your ground, in the land of which the LORD swore to your fathers to give you. The LORD will open to you His good treasure, the heavens, to give the rain to your land in its season, and to bless all the work of your hand. You shall lend to many nations, but you shall not borrow. And the LORD will make you the head and not the tail; you shall be above only, and not be beneath, if you heed the commandments of the LORD your God, which I command you today, and are careful to observe *them*. So you shall not turn aside from any of the words which I command you this day, *to* the right or the left, to go after other gods to serve them.

Deuteronomy 28:1–14

What a list of blessings! The Lord wishes to bless every aspect of our lives. There is no area of our lives that he does not desire to bless. And he asks us to choose his blessing.

Whereas it only takes fourteen verses to list the blessings of the Lord, it takes fifty-one verses to list all the

Joyce A. Howard

curses. These can be found in Deuteronomy 28:15–68. I challenge you to get a Bible and read through these scriptures. As you do so, try to recognize when, where, and how these curses still exist within our world. Please keep this thought uppermost in your mind: the Lord wants to set you free from the curse—or the effects of sin—which exist in your life. The Lord wants you to choose life!

The effects of the curse that can fall upon us when we fail to follow the Lord are many. Diseases are a curse. Slavery is a curse. Poverty is a curse. Living in a country without basic freedoms is a curse. There are aspects of widowhood that are considered a curse. There are factors related to having no offspring that are considered a curse.

Sexual Sin

I was sexually abused as a child. This happened more than once. In fact, it happened to one degree or another many times over many years. I am so thankful to the Lord that *none* of it was done by a member of my family, immediate or extended.

The incidents of sexual abuse began when I was around six years of age. They continued to occur throughout my college years. Sometimes they involved being sexually attacked. Other times they were exposure incidents I witnessed. Some of them I would term a form of sexual terrorism.

The first incident was the most traumatic for me, for more than the obvious reason of it being the first. After I got loose and ran home, I came in the house crying, desperate for comfort and security. I needed to be sheltered and told I was lovable and that I had done nothing wrong, that it had been done to me. I needed an adult to stand up for me and confront the perpetrator so that it never happened again.

Unfortunately, my mother was not able to do this for me. Instead she yelled at me and said it had never happened and that I should stop saying so. She walked away and left me there by myself. I remember sobbing quietly and saying to her, "But Mommy, look at my panties, look at my panties." Her denial and rejection of me at that critical juncture did more to harm me than the sexual attack itself had done.

Sexual sins are part of the curse. Sexual sins include adultery, abortion, defilement, deception (in regard to sexual sin), illegitimacy, divorce, fornication, sexual abuse, emotional abuse, physical abuse, exposure, homosexuality, lesbianism, frigidity, incest, incubus, succubus, seduction, alluring, masturbation, voyeurism, etc.[21] These effects of the curse are prevalent throughout our world. These effects were prevalent within my family.

I can remember over and over again, as abusive situations would occur, questioning God as to why. What was wrong with me? I sometimes felt as if I had a bull's eye marked on my forehead that signaled my location and availability. As an adult, I learned the effect of this curse was not just mine but was upon our whole family.

In talking with people involved in homosexuality, fornication, etc., I have been astounded to learn how many of them were sexually abused in their childhoods. Improper thoughts, urges, and desires were awakened in them at an inappropriate time and in an inappropriate manner. God created us as sexual beings with an appropriate time and place for that part of our being to be awakened. Satan knows that, and he tries to thwart God's plan through sexual abuse.

Earlier I discussed the concept of sin as a blocker to blessing. When our blessings are blocked due to sin, the result is that we experience some or all of these effects of the curse. Unremitted sin continues to be passed through the generations until it is recognized and someone repents for it and sets it right again with God. My cry to the Lord has been that I *not* leave a trail of unremitted sin after my life here on this earth is over.

Jesus loves us. He came to earth and freely gave his life so that we could be set free of sin. I am constantly awestruck by the love that Jesus displayed. He died so that your sins could be forgiven. He died so that my sins could be forgiven. All that is needed is that my eyes become fully open to the sin in my life; and when they do, that I freely and fully repent to the Lord Jesus for that sin. When I freely and fully repent with eyes and heart wide open before the Lord, I step back into his blessing, and I leave behind the effects of the curse that were being caused by my sin (or the sin of others).

I have asked the Lord to open my eyes to such sin. I am repenting and praying for all effects to end and for God's full blessing to return to our family. I am praying for God's full blessing for my siblings, our children, and our grandchildren. God is doing just that; it has been amazing to watch. Watch and see the goodness of the Lord. Two of my sister's daughters-in-law have joined the church, with one of them being baptized for the first time in her life. The marriages of our children are being restored and blessed. My granddaughter has been healed of hip problems she was born with. There have been other healings and blessings. God's blessings are so wonderful. I do not want to miss a single one of them.

We Must Awaken

In June of 2006 the Lord gave me a word concerning our need to prepare.

Now! Now! You must begin. Do not delay. Turn to me. Release your faith to me. Send your prayers as incense to my altar and the altar of my Son. Place a hedge around your families. Place a hedge around your church family and around your community. Place a hedge around all those you would want to be spared. The time to act is now. Too long you have slept. Too long you have allowed sickness and disease to come upon your people, my people. Too long you have waited until the manifestation was there. And then you awoke. Then you prayed, "Father, undo what has been done."

When will you awake, my children? When will you use the armor I have given you? When will you look ahead and see the storm gathering and protect against it? Clothe yourself. Clothe yourself in my righteousness. Arm yourself. Arm yourself in the armor I have given you. Use your shield as I designed it. Wield your sword as a mighty warrior. I have given you much. I have blessed you mightily. I have given all things unto you.

Awake! Awake now! Begin to pray now. Do not wait for the calamity to come. Watch. Get to the hills. Get to the outposts. Send out your scouts. Much is coming. And you must be prepared. Now is the time![22]

That is a powerful word! Jesus wants us to wake up and see what has happened to his body, the church. We have allowed sickness and disease to come upon ourselves and our loved ones. We have allowed inappropriate or failed relationships to exist. We have allowed bad decisions and improper thinking to exist. We have waited until the manifestation was there, and then we have asked the Lord to heal or deliver, to remove the manifestation. Jesus is calling us to be different. He wants us to come to the truth of his Word, to understand that healing, health, and wholeness are meant to be ours. Followers of Jesus should walk in total health, wholeness, and freedom. We should not be intimidated and controlled by the attacks of the enemy. Not if we understand his Word and use it as armor to protect us. Not if we clothe ourselves in his righteousness.

God's Plan for Your Life

Before the foundations of the world were created, God knew you. He set a plan in place for your life: a plan filled with the blessings of love, joy, peace, and all the fruit of the Spirit. It is a plan involving ministry and service to the Lord—right there in your everyday life. It is a beautiful plan based on intimacy with Christ and love of family and friends. You have a choice as to whether this plan occurs in your life or not. You can pray to discover God's plan and cooperate with the Spirit of the Lord to bring it to pass. Or you can choose to rebel against God and make your own decisions.

> I call heaven and earth as witnesses today against you, *that* I have set before you life and death, blessing and cursing; therefore choose life, that both you and your descendants may live; that you may love the LORD your God, that you may obey His voice, and that you may cling to Him, for He *is* your life and the length of your days; and that you may dwell in the land which the LORD swore to your fathers, to Abraham, Isaac, and Jacob, to give them.
>
> Deuteronomy 30:19–20

So far in my life, I have chosen a little of both of these. In most instances I have chosen life and blessing. But there have been times when I have gotten so wrapped up in myself, convinced I knew more than God, my parents, or my family, and tried to go my own way. These have, of course, been disastrous.

The Lord has been so gracious, slow to anger, and eager to forgive my transgressions. His grace and mercy have sustained me despite my own foolishness. I pray that you will continue to draw closer to the Lord. I pray that a continuous hunger for the Word of God will dominate your life. I pray that a deepening desire for service will fill your spirit. May Jesus be the way, the truth, and the source of life that guides and sustains you.

Joyce A. Howard

Letting Go of Fear

These past few years have been a time of tremendous conversion in my life. Letting go of fear has been one of the biggest changes I have experienced. I believe fear of rejection is a major stronghold in our world. It certainly was a stronghold Satan had upon me.

One of the ways the Lord uses to free me is through writing. I wrote the following in May of 2006.

Fear of being alone: left alone, unloved, unwanted, and unacceptable. This is what I have always feared. In the past, I would do anything to be accepted and loved. This is why I stayed in my first marriage, a marriage that I knew was not ordained of God. If I left, what would happen? Where would I go? Would I be alone? That was my fear. And so I stayed, even though I knew in my heart it was wrong. Even though I knew I was living a lie, even to my own family.

I did try. At different periods during the nineteen years I stayed, I made an all-out effort to make the marriage work. However, it was me trying to do it on my own; setting my will, trying to make it be right by sheer determination.

Growing up, living a lie was what our family did. We showed one face to the world—happy, successful, everything perfect—while the reality at home was quite different. It was ingrained in us to live that lie. No one knew that my parents drank and argued. No one knew there was dissension in the home. And we were all so naturally talented, God-given, that no one had reason to suspect. We were naturally intelligent and excelled at school. Some of us excelled at music and others at athletics of one form or another.

Mostly, we were natural leaders. When I look at my high school yearbook, I was not just in every club and activity, I was the president or secretary or treasurer or captain. I was voted the sweetheart of my senior class. My sisters and brother were all the same, with many accolades too. The fact that we were so naturally endowed with abilities made it easier to live the lie.

I remember as a young child arguing with God on Sunday afternoons about all of this, blaming God for the duality of our lives, our family life, my life. I always knew we were living a lie, and I hated it; I hated that God let it go on. Why didn't he just expose us? Why didn't he just show others what was going on?

Each of us individually tried to resolve the dichotomy. Some with money and recognition. Some with other things. Unfortunately, I grew up and started a lie of my own. This was what my first marriage was—full of dichotomy, duality. God forbid, even after I accepted Jesus into my life, the lie continued. All that changed was the content of the lie. I squeezed and pushed and forced my first husband to fit into the image of the new lie. Lord, I am so ashamed now by it all. I know that you understood. You knew why. You did not condemn me. Instead, you tried to help me see the truth.

I discovered the need to be set free of this fear of being alone—left alone, unloved, unwanted, and unacceptable—realizing this was Satan's main weapon that he had used against me since I was a small child and still can use against me even today if I let him. Seeing how I can be snared by this trap, constantly in need of the Lord to set me free. I see how this fear has kept me from being able to be quiet and alone (intimate) with you, Lord. I feared even your rejection, of being unlovable and unacceptable to you.[23]

I remember when I was a young girl trying to learn to ride a bike. My sisters and brother tried over and over to help me. But I just could not get over the fear of falling, the fear of failing at this simple task everyone around me could do. I was frozen in fear and unable to succeed. One day I decided I'd had enough. I decided I was going to ride the bike or else. We lived on top of a fairly steep hill. I got on my bike at the top of the hill and took off. I had determined I was going to ride the bike. If I did not succeed, well, I would suffer the consequences. Down the hill I went, screaming all the way. When I got to the bottom, I had to make the turn onto the highway and start pedaling as I did this. And it worked. I biked all the way up to the next crossroads and back. I could ride my bike.

A few years later, I remember trying to learn to swim. Again my family tried to help, and again I was frozen by the fear of failing. I could not let go of the fear long enough to be able to swim. Finally, I did the same thing I had done while learning to ride the bike. I had some friends take me out in the lake to deeper water and leave me. I either had to swim in or drown in the attempt. I swam in, and I swam successfully from that day on. (I do not recommend this method. I did this in Lake Huron.)

Most teenagers get their driver's license as soon as they turn sixteen. Not me. I successfully took and passed a driver's education class the summer before my sixteenth birthday, but I could not bring myself to go to the sheriff's office to take the written and driving tests. I kept putting it off, always having an excuse. It was the summer between my college freshman and sophomore years when I finally decided to battle that fear. Of course, I passed. It was never an issue of whether I could do it or not, just as with the biking and swimming. It was the power that this fear had in my life, the grip of this fear that kept me back.

Why? Why has fear of failing mattered so much? I know it was not the actual process it was linked to; that was simply where the fear got revealed. The underlying fear was, and always has been, *fear of rejection*. If I could not do this thing, whatever this thing was, would you continue to accept me? I am aware that this fear of rejection is a generational issue (curse) within our family. I know

Joyce A. Howard

it started when I was still sleeping in my crib. I can still remember (see myself in my mind's eye) rocking back and forth in the crib, sobbing, and intentionally banging my head against the top of the crib as I rocked.

I was the fourth child for my mother. When I was born, the other three were five and a half, three and a half, and one and a half. Mom and Dad had started out with nothing. They both had grown up during the Great Depression. Dad was sixteen, and Mom eleven when the stock market crash occurred, which precipitated the Depression. Shortly after marrying and starting a family, World War II broke out. My oldest sister was barely one when the Pearl Harbor attack occurred. During the years of World War II, my brother and another sister were born. I was born one month after the war ended.

Mom and Dad bought an old farmhouse on a wonderful parcel of land to fix up—no running water, no bathroom, and tons of work. The land upon which the house was located was rich for farming. Besides working full-time elsewhere, Mom and Dad planted potatoes for an additional income. The day I was born, Mom had to get Dad out of the field, as it was harvest time, to take her to the midwife's home where I was born. My aunts had to step in and feed the workers who were there that day harvesting the crop.

I know this does not excuse what happened, but I know it helps to explain it. It helps me to understand. My mom was not ready or capable of caring for another child at that point in her life. She did not have the faith needed to sustain her in the midst of her trials.

I have a grandson. He is the apple of my eye and also of his mom's and his dad's. He has a very sensitive soul, which is easy to see when you are around him. It was in looking at my grandson that I was able to understand some of what happened to me. You see, that is how I was. I needed constant assurance of cuddling and being held. My mother was not able to give it. That does not make my mother a bad person. She was not. It simply makes her a human being caught up in circumstances beyond her control. It makes her a member of Adam's race.

We are all born into a sinful world. Each of us is born a sinner, no matter how competent we are or how esteemed we are. It is the reality of our present world, whether we accept it as truth or not. Each of us needs a Savior. I did. My mother did. You do. It was not until I reached a crisis situation in my life in 1976 that I acknowledged this need and repented. Praise God, I was born again.

Since 1976, the Lord has been ever so patient with me. The reality is, even though I acknowledged I was a sinner and confessed my sin, I did not stop sinning that day. Even though he is slowly correcting areas of my life— thereby I am living a more Christlike life in those areas—I still sin. There are areas of my life that still have not come under redemption's light, Jesus' life, and love.

Loving God Without Fear

The Lord shared the following with me in May of 2006:

Daughter, I gave you this great love you shared with your husband. I saw the earnestness of your desire to know such

Joyce A. Howard

love, and I granted it unto you. Nothing will ever change that love you and your husband share. Do you not know it is eternal, everlasting? Do not doubt this. Your husband is here with me, and yet his heart holds all that memory and love he shared with you. Any wrongs are forgiven and forgotten. His love awaits your arrival in my kingdom.

Do you love your son? Do you also love your daughter? Do you love your son any less because of your daughter or your daughter any less because of your son? I know that you do not. One love relationship does not affect another love relationship, not when it is my love. There are no boundaries to my love; it stretches to places unfathomable to your mind; it has no beginning and no end.

Love me. Do not be afraid. Loving me freely and fully will not change your love for your husband or children or family or friends. Seek me. Be quiet with me. Come in the cool of the day. Come in the midst of your need. Come in the busyness of your job. Seek me and see me in every aspect of your life. See me as the answer to sin and weakness. I can free you from these. I can make you whole and capable.

Have no fears. Fear is not of me. Give me those fears. Bring them to my altar. I will crucify them and set you free. Believe in me. Believe in my love for you. I love you as a bridegroom loves his bride. I await you. Come! [24]

Jesus is ever so patient. He understands everything about us. He understands everything about me. When I make wrong choices, he knows everything about my life that caused me to do it. He does not condemn. Instead, he calls me in love to repent and heal. He ever so gently reveals to me the actions and choices I have made. He helps me to understand why I made them. He helps me to be set free to make better, wiser choices next time.

This call to be different includes the call to be healed of the effects of sin in our life. It meant that for me, and it does for you too. We are the product of a sinful world. God gave Jesus, his only Son, to save us. Jesus gave his life on the cross to make that happen. His blood redeems us. If you have never called on Jesus to save you, please do it now. Church attendance will not matter on judgment day. The Bible is clear: we are saved through repentance and belief in Jesus Christ. Do it today. *Do not let the hurts of your past control your tomorrows.* All things are possible through Christ Jesus, our Lord. Let him heal the hurts and wounds of your childhood. Let him make you whole.

Healing Relationships

I would like to share another area in my life that the Lord has graciously healed. Going away to college is meant to be a happy time, an exciting time. The evening before I left, I was busily packing. The college had sent a list of suggested items to bring, including practical items such as tape and paper clips and rubber bands. I was busily gathering these items. I could not find something I needed and so asked my mother about it. No doubt when I asked her, it was really the tenth or twentieth time I had asked her for something. No doubt my exuberance was annoying. I readily accept I was partially to blame.

My mother exploded. I mean exploded! She told me how she hated me, could not stand me, how I had annoyed her and bugged her since the day I was born. She told me she was glad I was finally leaving. Happy! And she said that her greatest hope was that I would never come back. In fact, she went on to say I was not welcome back. I should find somewhere else to go over the holidays. With that explosion, she went into her room and shut the door. My father tried to comfort me and tell me she had not really meant it. Unfortunately, I knew in my heart that a part of her did. It was what I had sensed and known intuitively, even as a baby. And it was the very thing Satan had been using against me since my birth: rejection.

The next day, we gathered to go. My oldest sister was helping with the transition, and I was told to go with her. My parents were arranging to pick up another of my sisters who was starting college with me. My mother managed not to speak to me that whole day. No apology. No good-byes. Nothing. My oldest sister could tell I was very sad, rather than happy and excited, to be heading to school. Upon her questioning and my explanation, she assured me that I would always be welcome at her home and that I should plan to come there for vacations.

So that is how my college experience began, with my mother's declaration of what I had suspected throughout my life. What Satan had tried to convince me of throughout my life. But God, in his goodness, had a surprise of his own. He gave me a born-again Christian roommate. Kaye truly became my lifeline during my first months at college. Her friendship, love, and acceptance sustained me and helped me to blossom. Kaye is still a special and important part of my life today.

My mother and I were able to become friends as she grew older and needed us to help care for her. Before she died, I knew she loved me, and she knew how much I loved her. I know now (I have received enough healing so that I recognize) that she did love me, even as a child; circumstances and sin just kept that from showing through at times. Every mother loves her child. I do not believe it is possible to not love a child you have nurtured and carried in your womb.

The Bible tells us that life is a gift from God. There are no accidents, no mistakes. Each of us was created on purpose by God. We were created at the right time in history to the parents God meant for us to have, even if we lack understanding of why. I was created on purpose by God. "For we are His workmanship, created in Christ Jesus for good works, which God prepared beforehand that we should walk in them" (Ephesians 2:10).

If sin and circumstances have kept you from fully experiencing the love of a parent, give that to Jesus. He is waiting to heal you and make you whole. He will give you his assurance that you were not created by accident. He will fill you with that love and life that were missing in your childhood. Nothing is too difficult for the Lord.

If there is anger, unforgiveness, or bitterness in your heart due to the circumstances of your childhood, give all of that to the Lord. Joy and peace and life will come from letting go of those things. They are like cancers that eat at your soul. We all understand how bad physical cancers are. We know when we see cancerous growths on someone's body that they are evil, not of God. Neither are anger,

Called to Be Different

unforgiveness, and bitterness; they are just as harmful or perhaps even more harmful than physical cancers.

I have forgiven both my mother and father for the mistakes they made in their lives. I have asked the Lord's forgiveness for the mistakes I have made in my life. I cannot expect Jesus' total forgiveness without offering the same to the others in my life. I understand that my parents were subject to the sin of this world. They too were in a battle with Satan and the effects of sin. I carry some of the scars of their battle. I am in that battle too, and my children, sisters, and family carry scars of my battle, especially my children.

I have come to understand that the hurtful experiences (like when I left for college) were not orchestrated by my mother to cause harm to me. They were mistakes that were made that I can forgive. They were mistakes that I was also partly the cause of (I must accept my part in what happened) and for which I can be forgiven. Offering forgiveness and seeking forgiveness frees me to move on to experience a greater level of peace and joy in my life. The weight of the sin is released, a weight that has been holding me captive. My mother had no idea what an effect that event (when I left for college) would have on my life. She did not do it to intentionally set me up to make wrong choices and fail. It is so important that we recognize the impact our sin can have on the others in our lives.

Through the years I have realized (no doubt, to a small degree) how my sins have impacted my sisters, my children, my nieces and nephews, and my grandchildren. At various points, I have gone to them to seek their forgiveness. I have no doubt that I will need to do lots more of it. What

Joyce A. Howard

I hope and pray for every day is that the cycle of sin will be broken in our family. I do not want sins committed by earlier generations of our family negatively impacting me, my children, or my grandchildren. Nor do I want sins that I have committed to have such an impact. I do not want any of these sins impacting my sisters and their families.

We have allowed Satan too much space and glory in our families. We have given him room to negatively impact the future generations of our families through our actions. My choice is to close the door to this. Let us decide that Satan will no longer be able to use us, through bitterness and unforgiveness or through unconfessed sin, to wreak havoc in our families. Let us instead choose to allow Jesus' blood to cleanse us and make us whole. Let us choose to allow Jesus' forgiveness and mercy to reign in our homes and lives. Let go of false humility, which is pride. Allow yourself to be humble and to seek forgiveness of others. Allow yourself to be humble and accept the forgiveness of others.

The greatest weapons that Satan has been able to use in my life have been rejection and sexual sin. He started using these against me when I was a small child. I have learned that when there are openings for Satan in our lives—through generational issues—he can visit small children, children far below the age of reason and account-ability, and bombard them. He does this to try to close the door to God's plans and promises for their lives.

Small children do not understand these attacks. They are unable to verbalize the attacks, or are afraid to verbal-ize them, and are unable to defend against them. I have spoken to several adults who have suffered from homosexuality issues. Each one has told me these thoughts began to torment them as very small children. I had one person tell me that he knew he was homosexual because he had these thoughts and urges from a young age, his earliest memories. Thoughts of rejection are my earliest memories. Does that make me unacceptable?

We need to see how Satan is attacking the young in our families and communities. We must pray to stop this. We must pray over babies and young children for protection for their whole being, spirit, soul (mind, will, and emotions), and body. We must plead the blood of Jesus over them. We must place a hedge of protection around them. Jesus is calling each of us to change the condition of our family. We are called to heal the relationships within our families.

Learning How to Love God

Abraham's Journey of Faith

Genesis 14:19–20 tells about Abram and when he first gave his tithe to the Lord:

> And he blessed him and said: "Blessed be Abram of God Most High, Possessor of heaven and earth; And blessed be God Most High, Who has delivered your enemies into your hand." And he gave him a tithe of all.
>
> Genesis 14:19–20

Called to Be Different

I find much comfort in reading about Abraham's life. To begin, he was seventy-five years old before he encountered the Lord, and the Lord called him to leave his family. Abram, as he was called at that time, was a descendant of Noah through Shem. Despite his being Noah's descendent, it still took him seventy-five years to begin to encounter the Lord. I find hope in that!

I do not know if Abraham was raised with an understanding of God through his heritage. What I do learn through reading the scriptures is that his revelation of God grew. It was several years after he began his journey with the Lord before there is a mention of his tithing to Melchizedek. And then more time went by before God called him into covenant. At ninety-nine years of age, God changed his name and taught him about circumcision. He was one hundred years old when Isaac was born.

During those twenty-five years, from his call to the birth of his son, we are told of two separate incidences where Abraham told his wife, Sarah, to lie and say she was his sister. In both cases, the Lord forgave him. At eighty-six years of age, he agreed to have sexual relationships with Sarah's maid, Hagar, giving birth to Ishmael. Ishmael became the father of the followers of Islam, giving rise to the Arab-Israeli conflict that still exists in our day.

It comforts me to know that Abraham, the great father of our faith, made mistakes. He did not have a sudden revelation of God and knew everything there was to know about the Lord. He grew in his knowledge and faith. He grew in wisdom. He made mistakes along the way, even serious mistakes that still plague his descendants and bring destruction throughout our world. This helps me to accept my humanity and know that God is not expecting me to live a perfect life. I am saved through Jesus. He calls me to grow in knowledge, faith, and wisdom, as Abraham did. But he is also ready to forgive me when I fall down and make mistakes. He cleanses me through his blood.

Earlier I shared the experience of my childhood. Blaming God and not accepting responsibility continued throughout my life, even after I accepted the Lord into my heart and received the baptism of the Holy Spirit. In January of 1983 I went on an eight-day silent retreat. My days were spent in silent reflection and prayer. The only times I was allowed to speak were during my once-a-day meeting with my spiritual director and during the evening meal.

In the early morning hours of the last full day of the retreat, I went upstairs into a tiny, soundproof chapel that was available to us for individual prayer. It was then that I got in touch with my tremendous anger at God. Out came the anger about my childhood. Out came the anger about my teenage years. But mostly out came all the anger about my first marriage.

The marriage was quickly performed by a justice of the peace because I was pregnant. The fall of my junior year of college, one of my friends was dating a member of the college's football team. He was also a member of a fraternity. So that we could double-date and have fun, I agreed to date another player who was a member of the same fraternity. When homecoming came, it turned out that all the couples were going to go to a motel to party all night. I ended up pregnant as a result of the event.

I fully accept this was my fault, my sin. No one forced me to go to the motel and be sexually involved. And I say this as if it was a one-time event, which it was not, as I continued to be sexually involved. It just happened that I became pregnant the first night.

Obviously you can see that God was nowhere in the picture for me at that time in my life. Well, not entirely. I had my roommate, Kaye, who tried to speak into my life. The trouble was, I was having so much fun that I did not want to listen. As for prayer, reading the Bible, or church attendance, they were not happening; they had not happened since I started college two years before.

So in January of 1983, seven years after I gave my heart to the Lord, I found myself in this isolated chapel in the middle of the night, getting in touch with my anger toward God. When I finally allowed the tomb in which I had successfully hidden and buried all this anger about my marriage to pop open, I exploded! I beat the floor with my fists and my feet. I screamed and shook and cried for what seemed like forever. I told God how I felt about everything that had occurred during the marriage. As it went on and on, I felt as if it would never end and that there would be nothing left to me when it ended.

But it did end, and finally I stopped shaking and crying. And as I lay there, face down on the floor of the chapel, for the first time in my life, I heard the voice of the Lord. I am not certain if it was an audible voice, although it certainly seemed like it was at the time. Jesus said these words to me, "I never asked it of you." They were said with such love that it is hard to find words to express how

I felt. That is all he said, but it truly transformed my life. I left that chapel a totally changed person.

The next morning, the last morning of the retreat, I went into the retreat center bookstore. I bought a bookmark with the serenity prayer on it: "God, grant me the serenity to accept the things I cannot change, courage to change the things I can, and wisdom to know the difference." On the back of the bookmark, I wrote, "Retreat '83 and continuing…" I still have that bookmark, and I am still continuing in that change.[25]

I told you about this incident so that I could discuss Jesus' commandment: "And you shall love the Lord your God with all your heart, with all your soul, with all your mind, and with all your strength" (Mark 12:30a).

Until I got rid of the bitterness and unforgiveness that I had stored up in my heart toward God, I could not learn to love him. This was a process I was going through during the retreat. It began with coming to terms with my life and letting go of the anger, bitterness, and unforgiveness. Again, God used my writing to set me free.

I wrote this reflection on the second day of the retreat: "I grew up blamed… and I accepted the punishment. I became so well trained that when no one else was there, I would blame myself… and punish me. Sometimes it is easier to be at fault than it is to be free."[26]

Two days later I wrote this: "Gently, sweetly, being, freeing, helping me to pass beyond. Ah, that is your love! To see the pain, to let it go free. How do you perceive me? Is it just your eyes that see? From heart to heart, acceptance comes to free. Freeing love: giving, being, letting go;

open-ended. What do you ask of me in return? Just to be free, to be, to see. To free the man I meet, good news of love breaking out, taking his captivity away, giving him sight, free to be. Freeing, giving love, always expanding, proceeding, being. Sweet gift of Jesus, Savior that you are, lover of mankind and me."[27]

On the sixth day of the retreat, I wrote the following: "Falling away, crushed, then flamed, burning into ashes and soot: walls so carefully constructed, the barriers of my heart. Let no more pain enter! My decision so long ago, shut off not to feel rejection's sting. Yet you have called me and I see. I must see if I am to live. Vulnerable, on a cross, freely accepted death to love. Jesus, my love, help my barriers fall. May I freely accept even death, death to all barriers that keep me from love."[28]

The Lord Jesus sovereignly met with me during those eight days. I believe he had been waiting for me my entire life to reach out to him, to seek his healing love. Those eight days were truly a turning point in my life. I wrote the following three days after this conversion experience: "Awakening to the brightness of new life, glistening of dewdrops, sunlight, and soaring birds, sweet odors of a new morn. Its freshness touches my being as gentle breezes soothe my skin. Such joy and peace created within me! Jesus reaching out to my world, re-creating; I am transformed by the power of his love. May my awakening now bring you life!"[29]

It was after this time that my love for the triune God began in its fullness. Not long after this, I wrote in my journal how I could now conceive of God as my Father:

"I feel so comfortable as his daughter now. Somehow I know the forgiveness I experienced was his, from him, my Father. Dad! As I feel at home as his daughter, I am now feeling a new revelation of Jesus' sense of his sonship and his identity with God as his father. There is such a strong desire within me to be consumed into the vastness of the universe, to be one with all creation, and for union and unity with all God is."[30]

Our God is a God of love. All love comes from him. He not only loves us but wants us to love him in return. Jesus understood what caused me to be unable to truly love him. He was ready and waiting to heal me. He is ready and waiting to heal you too. Accept his call.

The Many Touches of My Savior

In the dictionary, *covenant* is defined as a solemn agreement that is binding on all parties. [31]It is a formal and legally binding agreement or contract. *Covenant with God* is defined as the promises that were made in the Bible between God and the Israelites, who agreed to worship no other gods. [32]*To agree in covenant* is defined as to promise something in a covenant. [33]

I am reminded of something I heard Patricia Beall Gruits preach in March 2007.[34] She talked about the many touches that she had experienced from the Lord during her life. She said that this is how we should expect our life with the Lord to be—a deepening experience with key "touches" along the way, moments of further conversion that become major turning points in our lives. They are not so much times when God touches us as they are moments when we are actually able to reach out and touch the Lord, as when the woman with the issue of blood was able to touch the hem of Jesus's garment (Mark 5:25–34).

When I gave my heart to the Lord in 1976, I touched the Lord and entered into a covenant with him. I repented of my sins and gave the whole of my life to him. In return, Jesus and the Father came to live in my heart through the Holy Spirit. In response to my earnest prayer, I was baptized in the Holy Spirit at that same time, with the evidence of speaking in tongues. The gifts, fruit, and blessings of the Holy Spirit began to manifest themselves in my life.

On the retreat in 1983 I was again able to touch the Lord. It was a tremendous time of repentance and conversion. It was a time of opening to the love of the Lord. It was a point in time when my relationship with the Lord leaped to a whole new level.

Another major touch of the Lord occurred in March of 2005 with the decision to seek the Lord once again for Ted's healing. I shared earlier the role my college roommate played in his healing. It was at this time that a whole new dimension of the Lord's blessing began to manifest in my life; the Lord's healing power became real to me.

When Ted and I prayed for forgiveness on July 15, 2005 (two days before his death), I "touched" the Lord.

I felt another touch from Jesus at the time of my husband's earthly death/heavenly homecoming. When he manifested his presence to me the evening of the funeral, a deep and abiding trust in the Lord was birthed within me.

Another touch, or moment of further conversion,

occurred when I was water baptized in April of 2006. I was freed from the dominion and bondage of sin.

Another turning point for me occurred when I began to attend a new church in March of 2007. This is when I heard Pastor Gruits preach her message on the touches of the Lord.

I expect there will be moments of further conversion for as long as I continue to walk this earth. This is part of God's call to be different. This is part of God's blessing. I feel certain that as you were reading through these "touches" that occurred in my life, the Lord has been revealing to you times of such conversion in your life. Allow him to do so.

Our Final Conversion

When my husband passed away, I had stepped out of the bathroom for a moment. I think of how good he looked and responded to me just before I left the bathroom. He was breathing fine, his fever was gone, and he was fully responsive. If you had told me right then that he was about to depart from his earthly body, I would not have believed you. And he still looked so good (healthy, peaceful) when I came back into the bathroom. At first I had no idea he had departed.

It was so amazing to look at his earthly body, minus his soul (mind, emotions, and will) and his spirit. It was at that moment that I fully understood that *eternal life is real*. I had always believed in it, believed that my parents and brother were in heaven. However, there was something special about seeing this man I loved so dearly enter into eternal life that forever settled the issue for me. I hope and pray I can somehow convey this reality to you; my husband never died! He is more alive now than he ever was on this earth! He is more alive than we are! John records Jesus' question to us: "And whoever lives and believes in Me shall never die. Do you believe this?" (John 11:26).

Lessons on Love Through the Blessing of Children

The blessings of children and grandchildren are the greatest blessings the Lord has given to me. They are the means through which God has taught me about his love. Despite how my first marriage occurred, there was never a doubt when it came to the acceptance and love of my son. He was the Lord's gift to me in the midst of my disobedience and sin. He was Jesus calling out to me, displaying to me his tremendous gifts of love and forgiveness. My daughter was just such a gift. She too represented God, my Creator, sharing the gifts of life and love with me.

Despite the fact that my first marriage ended in a divorce that I helped cause, I am glad that it occurred. Without it, I would not have my wonderful children and grandchildren. My son and daughter mean so much to me. Those of you with children will know what it is I am trying to express, a bond that is so strong that it is almost inexpressible.

Without my first marriage, I would not have learned to reach out to Jesus for salvation. I made many mistakes during that first marriage and during the years that led to the divorce. Many times I have wanted to condemn myself for those mistakes, as others have condemned me. But Jesus has assured me of his forgiveness. His blood was shed to bring forgiveness to all those who call upon his name, who repent, ask for his forgiveness, and turn from their sins.

That does not excuse the mistakes I made. As I have already mentioned, our bad choices impact the "others" of our lives. My greatest concern has been, and will continue to be, the impact that my sins have had upon my children and grandchildren. Jesus assures me his blood is enough, that my faith and trust in him are enough. Praise God!

God has been true to his word in my life, working all things for my good (Romans 8:28). My Father loves me. Jesus loves me. Their love calls to me. It calls me to change. It calls me to turn over my life more and more to the Spirit of the Lord. *Jesus loves me so much that he will not leave me the way he found me.* He loves you in this same way.

Recognizing God's Gifts

After Ted passed away in 2005, I began praying and listening to determine what God's plan would be for me. During that next year, he spoke to me about the gifts he had placed in my life.

Gift of Thankfulness

At Thanksgiving 2005, he revealed his gift to me of thankfulness. He used my writing to do so. This was my greeting to my family and friends, just four months after Ted's death.

We have so much to be thankful for. There are so many of you who have touched my life in one fashion or another, and I am so thankful for you. I have realized this year, more so than ever, that the greatest blessings in life are the people that inhabit it. With my husband's death, the Lord has reawakened many friendships that were slowly ebbing on the shores of time. I am most grateful for that.

Often, I have joked with family and friends that I feel like I have lived several lifetimes in this one life. There are friends who have been with me since my elementary and high school days. Memories of those times do not fade, even when the friendships seem to wane. I guess maybe it is more like an ebb and flow. I am glad we have been making the effort to see each other and stay in touch by e-mail. You are still very important to me. I hope we will always stay in touch, here and when we get to our permanent, true home in heaven. My first adventure after high school was college. I am so thankful that the Lord brought my roommates into my life. There is no end to the blessing they have been and are to my life. I thank our Lord every day for them.

Have the rest of you moved around as much as I have? It amazes me to think about it and all the truly great people God has dropped into my life in the process.

And then came Ted, bringing with him a heart full of friends, stories, pictures, prayers, and love. What an untold blessing they have been!

Another amazing blessing to me is how many of you entered my world because you helped with Ted's care. You came into our lives to provide a service but stayed to be our friend. Keep it that way, okay?

My life just seems to twist and turn. And with each move, the Lord blesses me with more friends to be thankful for. Maybe you started out as a colleague I taught with at the college or someone I worked with on a committee or you were part of an organization I belonged to or a student I taught. And yet you stayed to become more than an acquaintance; you became my friend.

I have been so blessed here where I live with neighbors who did not stay neighbors but who became friends to spend time with, tell stories, barbecue, and care for and about.

I think each of you would agree that the blessings of family are the most precious and special of the gifts the Lord gives us. Our children and grandchildren top that list. They are what life is all about. And then close behind come sisters, nieces, nephews, in-laws, grandnieces, grand-nephews, cousins, and all the others.

I have been praying for the past several months to see if the Lord might be calling me back into full-time ministry. Guess what the Lord shared with me? I called you into the mission field years ago; didn't you know that? Look at your life. Look at all the places and people I have sent you to. Did you think it was an accident you lived in so many various places? Those were the churches I was sending you to. Now, get with it! Take care of these people I have given you to minister to. You are to bless their lives as they bless yours.

And so here I am, letting you know how much you matter to my life. Someone, I cannot remember who, described life as a tapestry. To me, it is more like some kind of a fancy quilt. Each of you represents one of the squares within my quilt. Some of your squares are beauti-ful; they are full of life, love, joy, and connectedness. Some of your squares are getting a little thin and frayed, and we need to work on that. We need to do some patchwork. Rekindle. Share. If we do not "get with it," there is going to be a hole in my quilt, an empty spot in my life that *no one but you* can fill.

So in this season of thanksgiving, I give thanks to the Lord Jesus for each of you. *You* are the blessings of my life. My house, yard, flowers, job, vehicle, they are things. They allow me to make it through the day. But they are not my life, my world. They will not go with me into eternity. You will! And the Lord will be there waiting to greet us![35]

I believe thankfulness is a gift that the Lord wants to give to you too. I have shared what the Lord had me write to help you to reflect on your own life. What he reveals to you about thankfulness will be similar—and yet different.

I am thankful that the Lord has opened my eyes to see all the friends he has given me throughout my life. In fact, this seems to be occurring at an exponential rate these days. And that is how it should be. The closer we come to the return of the Lord, the closer we should be coming to one another. The Lord is knitting us together into his bride. His yarn is love. His garment is praise. We are each called to be a part of his bride and to be prepared for his arrival. Praise to our Savior and soon-coming king, Jesus Christ!

Gift of His Life

Another month went by. The Lord gave me another message to share with family and friends concerning Christmastime.

Christmas is not about Christmas trees, Christmas decorations, Christmas lights, wreaths, or wrapping paper. Christmas is not even about Christmas gifts. Christmas is about the birth of a Savior. Christmas is about God's decision to bridge the gap between himself and man so that we could walk in fellowship with him.

God the Father missed the relationship he had with his first earthly family, Adam and Eve. Only in a few instances during time did God get to re-experience that relationship with man with such greats as Noah, Abraham, Joseph, Moses, David, Joel, Daniel, and Job, to name a few. I am sure those relationships were helpful, but...

Those of you who are parents can probably recall times when you have been in good standing with your children and then times when things were not going so well. It is a hard place to be, isn't it? To have to stand on the sidelines and watch your child struggle and sometimes suffer. Now try to imagine yourself as the father (parent) of the whole human race. I, for one, know I could not deal with it. Just me, I know I have caused God enough anguish as a parent that I shudder when I think about it. Now compound that by how many people?

So Jesus came. He came from heaven knowing and accepting that part of his coming would be that he would have to suffer and die. He came knowing he would have to be born as a baby, grow, be vulnerable, and be challenged. He came knowing he would have to grow to understand who he was and what his destiny was.

Once he was born, he did not know he was God. Imagine that! He had to agree to come, believing he would figure it out. He had no real idea what it would feel like to be a human being. He had to learn to crawl, walk, speak, and pray. He had to learn what it meant to walk by faith, to believe in that which could not be seen. It blows my mind that he would agree to all that!

Jesus came knowing he would be subject to the same human situation you and I live in. He came knowing that he would be tempted. He came knowing that he would have to overcome doubts, unbelief, sickness, and just sick ideas. He did not come full of faith. He had to discover and develop that faith in God the Father—his Father, my Father, your Father. That gives me such hope that I can do the same and that my children and grandchildren can do it, that you can too.

So this Christmas season, I send you greetings of hope and joy. Yes, each of us has experienced struggles and losses this past year. Those are inevitable, but they are not the last word. There is so much more of life yet to go. I write these words not just from me, but in memory of my husband. He wants you to know that there is so much yet to come, so much good we need to focus on that is coming our way.

My husband has moved on to our real life. He has shed his earthly body. He is experiencing a greater quality of life right now than we have ever experienced. This is so for other members of our family and friends. It will be true for more of our family and friends this next year. We need not despair, for that is really our goal. That is God's goal for us, God's plan. He sent Jesus to destroy death.

As a believer, I know I will someday shed this earthly body. My spirit (my true being) will rise into heaven, where

I will be greeted by my Father, God, and by my brother and Savior, Jesus. And I will be greeted by my husband and by other family and friends who have gotten to move on before me. I will be the healthiest, happiest, and freest I have ever been. It will be better than the best thing I can imagine or experience here on this earth. Praise God![36]

Along with that word on the meaning of Christmas, God gave me this scripture to share with everyone about God's gift of his Son.

> For God so loved the world that He gave His only begotten Son, that whoever believes in Him should not perish but have everlasting life. For God did not send His Son into the world to condemn the world, but that the world through Him might be saved. "He who believes in Him is not condemned; but he who does not believe is condemned already, because he has not believed in the name of the only begotten Son of God. And this is the condemnation, that the light has come into the world, and men loved darkness rather than light, because their deeds were evil. For everyone practicing evil hates the light and does not come to the light, lest his deeds should be exposed. But he who does the truth comes to the light, that his deeds may be clearly seen, that they have been done in God."
>
> John 3:16–21

Gift of Teaching

I love teaching. It is a gift God blessed me with as a small child. In early elementary school, the lessons were not challenging for me, so I was one of the first to complete my assignments. It did not take long for my teachers to realize they could use me to help other students. I helped others learn to read, write, and do math and geography. It was fun. I loved helping the other students. The desire to teach was birthed within me at that early age and is still in me today.

I have taught in one capacity or another throughout my adult life. I have been teaching at a community college since 1991. The Lord has given me many opportunities to witness and pray one on one with students, faculty, and staff at the college. I have come to realize that a key part of his plan is that I recognize and use this gift of teaching for his glory. In May of 2006 the Lord gave me this word concerning my job:

This is the season when you will witness to your students and bring many to me. This is the time of my harvest. I have placed you at the college for this season. You have been patient. You have let your life witness to me and to my fullness. You have built trust among many. They know you are real and that they can come to you. They know of your care and lack of condemnation through my grace.

Now is the harvest for all the seeds you have planted. Even former students will seek you out, for they know they can put their trust in you. You have shown them, through your life and your care of your husband, what it means to be my true follower. You do not need to reach out. They will come to you in my name and through the guidance of my Spirit. My sheep hear my voice and learn how to follow.

Be ready. Be prepared. I am shaking. Many will come. Let my Spirit guide your responses. It is only through me, not you. Yes, your fellow faculty and workers from across the college. And yes, your students, both past and present. Praise my name for the works I am doing![37]

What a blessed time we are living in. How blessed we are to be alive. Not just to observe, but to participate in the greatest harvest of souls for the Lord. This was spoken over me at MorningStar Ministries in September 2006:

You are gifted in teaching. You have the ability to take the difficult and make it simple. The Lord has given you this ability. You are to use it for the Lord and his kingdom.

The Lord is pleased with you. You have passed through a great tribulation and have overcome. You have passed the test. Other doors are now opening for you. Remember, the Lord will sustain you; do not try to do it in the natural. As you pass through these open doors, remember that his strength is made perfect in your weakness.

Depend on him and not yourself. As you are bold for the Lord, he will step in and help you. But you must step out. Salvation and deliverance belong to the Lord. He will rescue you at the right time.[38]

Although I know it is the Lord who gives these words to people, it still amazes me when total strangers can speak so clearly into our lives. Since these people had never met me, they had no way of knowing in the natural that I was a teacher. When they spoke that God said I had overcome and passed the test, I knew immediately that the tribulation to which they were referring was my husband's illness and death.

The Lord did not make Ted ill so that he could test us,

but we were tested as we walked through his illness and death. Would we remain faithful? Would we maintain our trust in the Lord despite how circumstances appeared? Would we continue to love each other and love the Lord? Would we believe in the Lord's goodness?

Gift of Writing

In December 2006 this was spoken over me at MorningStar Ministries.

The Lord has been showing you things. You need to write down what the Lord shows you in the Spirit. You need to be a good steward of God's word to you. What the Lord shows you is to be given to others. He shows it to you to be shared through you to the body, his church.

The Lord has given you the ability to break through in the Spirit. You are a breaker. Even as you speak a word, changes occur in the Spirit realm. Do not doubt this. Believe in your ability to break through. It has nothing to do with your voice or how loudly you pray but with the words you decree.

I see you like Joan of Arc. She changed the whole country through her beliefs and her words. You have her anointing. [39]

The Lord has given me an ability to express myself through writing. On my job, I have helped to write exposure control manuals, the lab manual my students use, a study guide for the students, etc. (Each time, there were others involved in the writing, with me often functioning in the role of lead author.)

In my personal life, I have written a short book on my husband's life (with the help of my sister-in-law, Riky), plus many short stories of how the Lord has blessed and worked through my life.

I believe this is one of the gifts the Lord wants to develop further in my life.

Gift of Faith

The Lord has given me the gift of faith. Faith both comes to us and increases through the revelation of the Word of God in our lives. Paul tells us, "So then faith *comes* by hearing, and hearing by the word of God" (Romans 10:17).

"For by grace you have been saved through faith, and that not of yourselves; *it is* the gift of God," (Ephesians 2:8). We must step out in faith even to accept Jesus as our Savior. And once we have done that, we must walk by faith in all that we believe and act upon.

God sees us as sinless because of the blood of Jesus and through our faith in Jesus. The book of Hebrews tells us: "But without faith *it is* impossible to please *Him,* for he who comes to God must believe that He is, and *that* He is a rewarder of those who diligently seek Him" (Hebrews 11:6).

Through faith, the petitions we make to the Lord are answered; we do not need evidence in order to believe. Again, it is the book of Hebrews that tells us, "Now faith is the substance of things hoped for, the evidence of things not seen" (Hebrews 11:1).

Through faith, we expect to receive what we ask for *before* it manifests. These are Jesus' words to his disciples:

"And whatever things you ask in prayer, believing, you will receive" (Matthew 21:22). We must believe Jesus and his Word. We must pray with belief.

I love the book of Hebrews, especially chapter eleven. In it, Paul recounts for us the heroes of our faith: Abel, Enoch, Noah, Abraham, Sarah, Isaac, Jacob, Joseph, and Moses, with mentions of Joshua, Rahab, Gideon, Barak, Samson, Jephthah, David, and Samuel. All of these giants of our faith believed God and prayed with expectant faith. Paul concludes, "And all these, having obtained a good testimony through faith, did not receive the promise" (Hebrews 11:39). Paul tells us that these great men and women of faith did not see the full manifestation of what they had been promised and had believed in. That is a powerful word to us if we will but hear and comprehend it. Our hope is in the Lord, who brings the physical manifestation of the answer to our prayers. Paul continues in Hebrews 12, exhorting us:

> Therefore we also, since we are surrounded by so great a cloud of witnesses, let us lay aside every weight, and the sin which so easily ensnares *us,* and let us run with endurance the race that is set before us, looking unto Jesus, the author and finisher of *our* faith, who for the joy that was set before Him endured the cross, despising the shame, and has sat down at the right hand of the throne of God.
>
> Hebrews 12:1–2

All of God's promises are obtained by faith. Paul exhorts us over and over in his Epistles to run the good race of

Joyce A. Howard

114

faith. In 1 Timothy, he tells us, "Fight the good fight of faith, lay hold on eternal life, to which you were also called and have confessed the good confession in the presence of many witnesses" (1 Timothy 6:12).

Ephesians 6 reminds us that faith is a shield that can both protect us and be used for defense: "Above all, taking the shield of faith with which you will be able to quench all the fiery darts of the wicked one" (Ephesians 6:16).

James 1 exhorts us, "But let him ask in faith, with no doubting, for he who doubts is like a wave of the sea driven and tossed by the wind" (James 1:6).

So whatever my need is, I must go to God through Jesus with no doubt or unbelief in my heart or mind. James also tells us, "And the prayer of faith will save the sick, and the Lord will raise him up. And if he has committed sins, he will be forgiven" (James 5:15).

We are told in Jude, "But you, beloved, building yourselves up on your most holy faith, praying in the Holy Spirit," (Jude 1:20). When we pray in tongues, we are building ourselves up in our faith. We are speaking mysteries to God for our own edification. It is a sustaining power that the Lord designed for us to have so that we could run and fight through faith.

I pray that my faith will guide me through his Word with inspiration from the Holy Spirit and through the people the Lord brings into my life to be my earthly guides. We are designed to be overcomers! We are designed to win the battles of our lives!

Gift of Love

I am a believer who also happens to be a science teacher. In science, we believe that the world is controlled by physical laws. There is a universal physical law known as the Law of Conservation of Energy.[40] This law states, "In any process, the total energy of the universe remains constant." Put simply, energy can be changed from one form to another, but it cannot be created or destroyed. The total amount of energy and matter in the universe remains constant, merely changing from one form to another. This law has become one of the most accepted of all basic laws of science.

Our Creator and Father built fundamental laws within this universe that he created. He did this in the physical realm of the universe. He also did it in the spiritual realm of the universe. When the Lord set Adam and Eve in the garden, he gave them basic laws they were to follow. Due to deception, sin entered the world.

The Lord has been on the move, correcting what went wrong. He began with Adam and Eve. He sacrificed an animal and used its skin to clothe them (Genesis 3:21). As time went on, God gave directions to his people, the Israelites, whom he had chosen. He taught them to sacrifice animals and to use the blood as atonement for their sins. He gave Moses the Ten Commandments to guide his people on how to live in harmony, both with him and with one another. All these things foreshadowed the plan that our Father had to send his Son to bring about redemption and the forgiveness of sins, once for all time.

Exodus records the giving of the Ten Commandments

from God through Moses (Exodus 20:3–17). The Ten Commandments were given for our good. They were meant to set the parameters by which we would live our lives in relation to our Father and in relation to one another.

But man took those Ten Commandments and turned them into hundreds of laws. They governed everything a person could and could not do. They determined the first words they were to say in the morning and the last words they were to say at night. They governed how they put on and took off their clothing, all in a prescribed order. They determined how they ate, what they ate, and where. There were even prescribed sleeping positions. Tossing and turning would have been considered a sin.

There were hundreds of laws that ruled the Sabbath. Depending on how you did it, spitting could have caused you to break the Sabbath law. As these laws were being developed, the Israelites thought they were going to be a help to them, that they would help them to keep the Ten Commandments. However, they were being deceived. In the end, they were bound and strangled by the laws of men.

As I looked at the scriptures concerning the commandments, I recalled Jesus' interchange with one of the teachers of the law. Jesus defined what he believed to be the summation of the commandments, centering it on love of God, and then flowing from that love, love of neighbor. Since Jesus is my model in all things, he is my model with regard to the commandments. I am trying to live my life in obedience to this greatest commandment, love, as given by Jesus.

The Gospel of Mark records what has become known as the greatest commandment:

Jesus answered him, "The first of all the commandments *is:* *'Hear, O Israel, the* LORD *our God, the* LORD *is one. And you shall love the* LORD *your God with all your heart, with all your soul, with all your mind, and with all your strength.'* This *is* the first commandment. And the second, like *it, is* this: *'You shall love your neighbor as yourself.'* There is no other commandment greater than these."

Mark 12:29–31

Gift of Praise

Paul exhorted the Philippians (and you and me) to praise God in all circumstances and situations. Even when we do not understand *what* is happening or *why* a particular event is happening, we are exhorted to praise. When we praise the Lord in the midst of trying circumstances, we are manifesting our faith, trust, and belief in a loving, merciful God. We are saying that despite how things may look on the surface, it is the Lord we are looking to. We are affirming that the controlling anchor of our lives is Jesus Christ. Paul wrote:

> Not that I speak in regard to need, for I have learned in whatever state I am, to be content: I know how to be abased, and I know how to abound. Everywhere and in all things I have learned both to be full and to be hungry, both to abound and to suffer need. I can do all things through Christ who strengthens me.

Philippians 4:11–13

Joyce A. Howard

King David knew how to praise God. If you have not had a chance to read the Psalms, I exhort you to do so. They are filled with praises. King David wrote this psalm to the Lord:

> The LORD upholds all who fall, And raises up all *who are* bowed down. The eyes of all look expectantly to You, And You give them their food in due season. You open Your hand And satisfy the desire of every living thing. The LORD *is* righteous in all His ways, Gracious in all His works. The LORD *is* near to all who call upon Him, To all who call upon Him in truth. He will fulfill the desire of those who fear Him; He also will hear their cry and save them. The LORD preserves all who love Him, But all the wicked He will destroy.
>
> My mouth shall speak the praise of the LORD, And all flesh shall bless His holy name Forever and ever.
>
> Psalm 145: 14–21

The hardest part for me has been to learn to praise God in the midst of dire circumstances. I have written how my husband went through over twenty-four hospital stays. Over and over, doctors would suggest that there was nothing more they could do and would recommend hospice. One doctor back in 1994, eleven years before Ted went to be with the Lord, told me that I needed to put him in a home. He was in a home—ours! How funny it seems that it took until we gave up on the doctors and medicine before the Lord began to heal his body.

I have experienced healing within family members and

myself, both through doctors and medicine and without their intervention. I consider both methods to be God's healing. I would never refuse to see a doctor unless I had an extremely strong unction from the Lord telling me so. We should believe for God to heal and then leave it to him to guide us to that healing.

Praising and worshiping the Lord is our privilege and our blessing. We are created to fellowship with our triune God—Father, Son, and Holy Spirit. If we only praise the Lord in the good times, what would that say about our trust in him? We must praise and worship him in spirit and in truth. We must praise him despite what we see. He is our Father, our shepherd, our comforter, and our friend. Let all that has breath praise the Lord!

A family member wrote the following to me as part of a discussion we were having on why we need to praise: "Where God is praised and glorified, Satan has to flee." This is what I pray we would do, that we would praise and glorify God within our families. I pray that we would ask our Lord Jesus to be present among us to heal us and to further his kingdom within our families. I pray that we will petition our Father God and our Lord Jesus to free our families from diseases, disorders, addictions, or other results of sin, so that our children and grandchildren can live without these hindrances.

Gift of Forgiveness

I have failed in my walk with the Lord. When I fail, I must bring that failure and sin under his blood. I must see that I have sinned and then confess the sin and ask his forgiveness. "If we confess our sins, He is faithful and just to forgive us *our* sins and to cleanse us from all unrighteousness" (1 John 1:9). I must put myself back into right standing with the Lord so that I can stay under the protection and blessing of his blood. I must allow him to cleanse me of my unrighteous thoughts, actions, and deeds.

> "Beloved, now we are children of God; and it has not yet been revealed what we shall be, but we know that when He is revealed, we shall be like Him, for we shall see Him as He is. And everyone who has this hope in Him purifies himself, just as He is pure."
>
> 1 John 3:2–3

I looked up the word *pure* in the thesaurus.[41] It has several meanings. First, it means to be unmixed—clean, untainted, unadulterated, clear, unalloyed, undiluted, natural, genuine, real, immaculate, unsullied, unpolluted, and pristine. Second, it means to be absolute—stark, sheer, downright, and thorough. Third, it means to be sinless—chaste, virtuous, "squeaky clean," decent, good, wholesome, moral, blameless, innocent, and guiltless.

When I look up words, I like to look up what their opposite means, as that always seems to help me to understand the word even better. The opposites of *pure* are impure, tainted, mixed, diluted, dirty, sinful, wicked, impure, and unchaste.

Since we are exhorted to purify ourselves as he is pure, I looked up the word *purify*.[42] This is what it means: clean, cleanse, sanitize, sterilize, clarify, purge, decontaminate, wash, filter, refine, or distill.

So this is what I will strive for. But in so doing, I must not forget that I am acceptable only through Jesus' blood and not my works. I cannot work my way to heaven. I will strive to do what is right, and I will strive to be obedient, but it is by God's grace that I am saved.

It is God's grace that is there when I fail. When I truly see my sin for what it is, repenting of it and asking the Lord's forgiveness and healing, he forgives me, cleanses me from all unrighteousness, and heals me. Looking at the Ten Commandments, I realize that during my lifetime, I have failed at nine of them. And if I consider what Jesus taught about the heart, then I have failed at all ten. Yet, my Father has forgiven me. He sees me only through the blood of his Son, my Savior, Jesus. My inner strength comes from Jesus and his Spirit; it is not something I can accomplish under my own power. "'Not by might nor by power, but by My Spirit,' says the LORD of hosts" (Zechariah 4:6b).

To truly be different for the Lord, we need to allow the Lord to show us the gifts he has placed within us. I hope that as you have read through the giftings God has shown me, you have allowed the Holy Spirit to begin to speak to you about the giftings he has placed in your life. If not, stop right now and take that time. Meditate on giftedness. Allow your father to speak to you.

Blessings through Tithing

We learn in the third chapter of Malachi:

> "Bring all the tithes into the storehouse, That there may be food in My house, And try Me now in this," Says the LORD of hosts, "If I will not open for you the windows of heaven And pour out for you *such* blessing That *there will* not *be room* enough *to receive it.* "And I will rebuke the devourer for your sakes, So that he will not destroy the fruit of your ground, Nor shall the vine fail to bear fruit for you in the field," Says the LORD of hosts; And all nations will call you blessed, For you will be a delightful land," Says the LORD of hosts.
>
> Malachi 3:10–12

Ted was the person whom the Lord used to teach me about tithing. Giving to the Lord of both his time and his money was just his nature. He did it willingly and freely, seemingly without thought.

2 Corinthians tells us:

> But this *I say:* He who sows sparingly will also reap sparingly, and he who sows bountifully will also reap bountifully. *So let* each one *give* as he purposes in his heart, not grudgingly or of necessity; for God loves a cheerful giver. And God *is* able to make all grace abound toward you, that you, always having all sufficiency in all *things,* may have an abundance for every good work.
>
> 2 Corinthians 9:6–8

Ted was raised within the Catholic faith. When he heard the call of God in his life, he responded by becoming a Catholic priest. When we made the decision to commit our lives to each other, it included the knowledge that he would no longer be allowed to function as a priest. It was an extremely hard decision for him, one that he wrestled with for quite some time. He truly felt called of the Lord.

I would like to share an experience I had with the Lord. The Lord gave me a vision of Ted in heaven. He showed me that he is a priest (minister) there. The Lord spoke these words into my heart, "My gifts and callings are irrevocable." It does not matter if the Catholic Church is currently of a mind-set that does not allow the marriage of priests. God's call is and was there, and it was not mistaken. Heaven is forever, and in heaven, Ted is fulfilling his call.

Joyce A. Howard

What exactly that means, I do not have the answers, but my trust is in the Lord. The church is imperfect, imperfect because it is made up of us, imperfect human beings. A hundred years from now, perhaps the Catholic Church will realize that being married is not an impediment. All that has occurred now will be forgotten. It is important we do not make our determinations based on the temporal.

Ted was diagnosed with MS one year after we married. His illness tried to overshadow our lives. It stretched our faith. We learned dependence on the Lord for time, energy, finances, etc. The Spirit of God saw us through multiple hospital stays and untold medical expenses. I believe the Lord was faithful to us because we were faithful in our giving to him.

We gave our tithes and offerings, we gave of our time and energy, and we gave out of our need. We did not retreat from God when we were in the midst of our trial. Instead, we pursued him more closely and depended on him more fully. We praised him in the midst of our struggles. We honored his name, and proclaimed his name and love to all our family and friends. We reached out to our neighbors in need. We gave, even of the limited money we had, to others. Our love for each other—a love that seemed to be of one whole, not two parts—we freely gave to others. Our love made us stronger.

The Lord's greatest blessing to us was that gift of *agape* love. I pray that it is a gift he will continue to bless me with throughout the remainder of my days here on this earth. *Agape* love is selfless and unconditional; it is love that loves in spite of, not because of. To walk in God's love is to walk in his kingdom.

"Bring back our captivity, O LORD, As the streams in the South. Those who sow in tears Shall reap in joy" (Psalm 126:4–5). This is the joy that I experienced throughout the trials and testing of Ted's illness. Many times I told people that I would never trade one moment of the time with my husband, despite the trials. This is the joy I experienced even as Ted left this earth to go on to his heavenly reward. I believe these blessings of love, joy, and peace that Ted and I experienced were the fulfillment of Malachi 3—the giving of our tithes to the Lord.

The Fruit of the Spirit

In the book of Galatians, we are exhorted to walk in the Spirit.

> I say then: Walk in the Spirit, and you shall not fulfill the lust of the flesh. For the flesh lusts against the Spirit, and the Spirit against the flesh; and these are contrary to one another, so that you do not do the things that you wish. But if you are led by the Spirit, you are not under the law.
>
> Now the works of the flesh are evident, which are: adultery, fornication, uncleanness, lewdness, idolatry, sorcery, hatred, contentions, jealousies, outbursts of wrath, selfish ambitions, dissensions, heresies, envy, murders, drunkenness, revelries, and the like; of which I tell you beforehand, just as

I also told *you* in time past, that those who practice such things will not inherit the kingdom of God.

But the fruit of the Spirit is love, joy, peace, long-suffering, kindness, goodness, faithfulness, gentleness, self-control. Against such there is no law. And those *who are* Christ's have crucified the flesh with its passions and desires. If we live in the Spirit, let us also walk in the Spirit. Let us not become conceited, provoking one another, envying one another.

Galatians 5:16–26

During the fall of 2006, the Lord led me to take part in a Cleansing Stream seminar and retreat.[43] The purpose of the seminar was to help believers to learn to walk in the Spirit. In the first lesson, we discussed justification and sanctification.

Justification happens in an instant through the Spirit. It occurs when we recognize our relationship with our Creator God—we are sinners in need of salvation through Jesus Christ. Through recognition of our sin and repentance (turning away from our former lives, turning toward God), we are born again into the family of God and justified. When we believe that Jesus died for our sins and accept what he did for us, we are saved. Through salvation, we are led to dedicate our lives to God, which is witnessed through water baptism. We are called to become baptized into the Holy Spirit through the laying on of hands, to receive the power of the Spirit to enable us to live our lives as followers of Christ.

Sanctification is the ongoing process of renewing our souls (our mind, will, and emotions) and our bodies. It is during this process that we learn to walk in God's Spirit, to be led by the Spirit, and die to the desires of the flesh. The flesh consists of the areas of our lives that have not as yet been renewed by the Word and the Spirit. The flesh includes thoughts that are not in alignment with God's thoughts, choices we make that are not in alignment with God's will, desires that are not submitted to God, and undisciplined areas in our bodies.

Keys to walking in the Spirit are trust in the Lord, obedience to his Word, and listening to the still, small voice of the Holy Spirit within us. We can assess how well we are walking in the Spirit by looking for evidence in our everyday lives. We do that by looking for the fruit of the Spirit in our lives: love, joy, peace, longsuffering, kindness, goodness, faithfulness, gentleness, and self-control.

The Fruit of Love

I first began to understand the truth of God's love through the birth of my children. This is one of the true blessings of the Lord; he shares his gift of birthing life so that we will understand the reality of true love. Not brotherly love, not erotic love, but the unconditional, God kind of love—*agape* love.

The God kind of love was made even more apparent through the birth of my grandchildren. It was then that I truly began to understand that family is the true inheritance of the Lord. God's blessing is in the life and love we share with our children and grandchildren and the truth of God's love that we make manifest in their lives.

As I shared earlier, this is the kind of love I experi-

Called to Be Different

enced with my husband, Ted. I cannot recall Ted being angry, raising his voice in an abusive manner, or speaking a negative word. I feel like I lived with Jesus, as Ted's whole life exemplified him.

The Fruit of Joy

Joy produces strength and brings healing. Joy was a gift that the Lord gave me in 1976 when I was born again. My heart was filled with such joy that I thought it would burst! That joy has never subsided. Joy is what helped me through the loss of my husband. It was then that the truths about grief and joy became reality to me. I first wrote about this experience in October of 2006.

Grief Is a Choice

Grief is a choice you can make throughout your life. Grief is a choice you can make in the lifelong relationship you have with a person who dies. The Bible is clear that there will always be seedtime and harvest. This is one of the great laws that God our Creator instituted on this planet.

When a person dies, all the seeds planted with regard to that person's life will come to harvest. It is a form of judgment, in that the results of the harvest are determined by the types of seeds that were planted throughout the life of the person. No doubt time will show that an inevitable combination of both good and bad seeds was planted.

There are three kinds of seeds that must be considered. First, those that were planted in your life that *indirectly* affected the types of seeds that were planted in the per-

Joyce A. Howard

son's life who died. Second are the kinds of seeds that were planted *directly* between you and the person who died. And third are the kinds of seeds the person planted throughout his or her life.

These are what we grieve. We grieve the fruit of the harvest. The good seeds of love, joy, peace, forgiveness, patience, etc., create a harvest of good fruit. Good fruit produces more good fruit, more love, joy, peace, etc. The bad seeds of hate, fear, discord, anger, bitterness, jealousy, etc., create a harvest of bad fruit. Bad fruit produces more bad fruit—eating disorders, dependencies (alcohol, cigarettes, drugs, etc.), other bad habits, cancer, sickness, more hate, fear, etc.

As I said earlier, most of us find a combination. We find some good fruit mixed in with some bad fruit. When we find good fruit, we experience the joy of the relationship we shared. We have positive memories of our life with that person. We feel joy because our loved one has reached his or her final destination: heaven. When we find bad fruit, we have two choices. We can choose to continue with the cycle of bad seeds producing bad fruit, or we can choose to repent. Grief can be a form of repentance.

First, the Spirit of the Lord may remind you of things you did or said in your life that *indirectly* negatively affected the life of the person who died. When this happens, you must stop and repent of it. From the depth of your being, you must ask forgiveness and cleansing.

Forgiveness: This involves forgiveness in relation to the person who died. Next, it involves a widening view of others, both alive and dead, where you have done the same thing. You must ask the Spirit of the Lord for forgiveness with regard to these others. And then you must let go and accept that forgiveness. This is a process over time.

Rightness: You ask the Lord to free you and heal you. You ask him to increase your spiritual insight so that you will not continue to do these same things in the future, that your words and actions will stop negatively impacting others. You ask the Spirit of the Lord to quicken your spirit and stop you short.

Second, the Spirit of the Lord may remind you of things you did or said *directly* to the person who died. The Spirit of the Lord reveals these to you so that you can repent of them and set right your relationship with the person. You ask forgiveness of that person through the Lord. It does not matter that he or she is already dead. In God, there is no time. God exists outside of time. Therefore, Jesus is the same yesterday, today, and tomorrow. This is our basis for inner healing; the Spirit of the Lord can re-enter any moment in our life, or the life of another, and set it right.

Third, the Spirit of the Lord may remind you of things that the person who died did or said in his or her life that are negatively impacting others. You can help to set this right. You can intercede on his or her behalf to correct or heal the effects of the wrongs committed by the person toward others. For example, you may be a sibling, and your parent dies. You see what the parent did that is negatively influencing and impacting the life of your sibling. Pray for rightness of the situation. Pray that your sibling will be set free from these negative influences caused by the parent.

Another example: You may be a grandparent, and your child dies. You see how the wrong choices your child made in his or her life are stifling the life of your grandchild. You can pray (intercede) for rightness of the situation. You can pray for your grandchild to be set free of the chains that are binding him or her. You are praying to reverse generational sin. "I lay the sins of the parents upon their children; the entire family is affected—even children in the third and fourth generations of those who reject me" (Exodus 20:5b, NLT).

Or you may be a spouse, and your spouse's parent dies. You see what the parent (or grandparent or sibling, etc.) did that is negatively impacting your spouse.

Every seed we plant will come to harvest. Seedtime and harvest are eternal, everlasting. That is why it is so important, so vital, that we understand the need for the Spirit of the Lord to be in charge of our lives. That is why it is so important that we live by the Spirit and walk by the Spirit.

God will not go against his own natural laws. You cannot plant seeds of doubt and unbelief and expect a harvest of healing and deliverance. Each of us will reap what we sow. "Do not be deceived, God is not mocked; for whatever a man sows, that he will also reap" (Galatians 6:7).

A life well lived will reap a harvest of righteousness and blessing and glory. Everyone connected to that person will reap the benefits. They will see God's love and goodness in action. This fact was so true for Ted. He was such a shining example of what a Christian's life and demeanor should be like. [44]

The Fruit of Patience

I pray you are experiencing the blessings of the Lord. Indeed, his call to us each day is to see, hear, experience, and enjoy those blessings, always recognizing that there are times those blessings come to us through difficulty, struggle, and trial. Blessings are often something God calls us to birth within us or to birth within our sphere of authority—family, church, neighborhood, community, workplace, etc.

God calls us to birth our blessings just as he calls us to birth our children. Women will especially understand this process. We know it had to begin through a joining together physically, as well as emotionally and spiritually.

Who better than a woman to know the ups and downs and struggles of the nine-month process of birth? Who better than a woman to understand the experience of the waiting, the joy of anticipation, and the fear of the unknown involved? Who better to understand the discipline involved in what to eat and drink, how to exercise, get proper rest, and have patience.

Who better to understand that birthing involves a total rearrangement and realignment of your priorities, values, goals, plans, and dreams. We know what it requires, all the time and energy involved in the preparation and the daydreams and anticipation involved. Ladies, we know what birthing means!

And then comes the main event: the actual birthing. The water breaks. The pain comes...and comes...and continues to intensify. Part of us says, "No! Stop! I don't want this!" But by this time, the birth is taking place. It cannot be stopped. And then comes the joy, the revelation of that new life, a totally new creation. Praise God! Part of us is exhausted from the process, while another part of us is so exhilarated that we can hardly stand it. Another part of us now fully realizes the implications of what we have birthed and is fearful whether we are up to the challenge. So many amazing thoughts and feelings occur at one time.

So here we are, sisters and brothers in the Lord, birthing one another, birthing deeper bonds to one another, and growing together in the Lord. We pray for, anoint, and support one another. We become prayer shields for one another. I am totally in awe. In my spirit, I feel we have only begun. I feel we are only starting to understand God's call to us. I feel the Lord is directing, guiding, teaching, and building us into his bride.

Where? With whom? Starting when? I want to know all these answers now. The Lord says it takes nine months in the natural to birth a child. Wait. *Be patient.* Does a child form all at once in the womb? Or is it a process? Are there steps and degrees and waiting involved? Does it require discipline and cooperation on our part? *Does a lord have to explain himself to his servants in order for them to be obedient?*

The Fruit of Gentleness (Meekness)

humbleness toward God

Gentleness (meekness) is another of the fruit of the Spirit. Meekness (*praotes* in Greek) is an attitude of humility toward God. It includes gentleness toward others, conscious choices based upon our recognition of God's love and mercy. Jesus spoke of meekness in his ministry, saying that those who are meek will inherit the earth (Matthew 5:5).

Pride (*huperephania* in Greek) is the very opposite of meekness. During the fall of 2006, the Lord showed me that I was being prideful. I was not consciously choosing to be prideful, but I was unwittingly being prideful. And in doing things with a prideful attitude, whether intentional or not, it was opening the door to the curse. The Lord kept bringing the expression "Proud to be an American" into my mind. It took many times of this happening before I finally caught on to what he was trying to show me. It had to do with discovering secret areas of pride in my life that were openings for the enemy.

This is an expression we were raised on: "Take pride in what you do and do it well." The Lord wanted me to see that he wanted me to be *thankful* that I was raised with a strong work ethic and moral ethic. These are areas to be thankful, not prideful.

Please understand that I was not even aware that I was being prideful. On our own, we cannot know we are prideful because the first ramifications of pride are in the areas of blindness and deception. The Lord wanted me to see that this is one of Satan's major strongholds in our world, especially in America. Satan causes us to be prideful in ways that we do not realize are happening. I, for one, am praying for the Lord to break that stronghold in my life. Only if the Lord breaks it and reveals the areas of pride to me can it be broken.

Another event happened during this time in which the Lord was showing me about the deceitful way Satan uses pride. I received something in the mail that I had ordered from Jim Bakker's ministry.[45] When I opened the package, it included a copy of a personal note from Jim Bakker thanking me for my support. As I held it, all I could think was, "Here is a truly humble man."

And then I realized Jim Bakker had been humbled. He was humbled in front of the whole world; he was sent to jail for fraud, he and his wife divorced, and he lost his entire ministry. In prison, Jim Bakker wanted to kill himself, causing the guards to have him on a suicide watch. After he had been there for quite a while, he got a visitor. It was Billy Graham.[46] Billy came to tell him that the Lord loved him and had forgiven him and that he needed to forgive himself. Billy helped him to come back from the brink, visiting him over a period of years.

When Jim was paroled from prison, it was Billy's son, Franklin, who was there to bring him to his home. Franklin Graham took him in, took him to his church, plopped him down in the front row with his family, and then announced his welcome to the congregation.[47] Franklin helped Jim to heal and come back. What a blessing! Restoration belongs to us in the Lord.

This is my point: I can choose to let the Holy Spirit reveal all hidden areas of pride in my life and pray to be cleansed of them, or I can let the enemy use them against me, and I can wait to be humbled. So I am thanking the Lord for showing me these hidden areas of pride in my life. I am thanking him that he has revealed them so that I might be set free.

I am *thankful* I was raised in a family with a strong work ethic. I am *thankful* I have been trained up to be a good teacher and a good grandmother. To the extent that I am capable and with the Lord's help, I am finished with hidden pride. I put it down. I no longer accept its presence in my life. I am asking the Lord to reveal it to me and heal and cleanse me so that these footholds for the enemy are gone from my life.

We each need to become more conscious of how deceitfully the enemy works in our lives. It is hideous, and it is unfair. But this is a real battle. We are in a spiritual battle for our lives, the lives of our families, our marriages, etc. Pride is the opposite of meekness.

God's Word Regarding Pride

I would like to share with you some scriptures associated with pride. These scriptures helped me to get a handle on areas that were negatively impacting my life and the lives of my children and grandchildren. Isaiah tells us about the origin of Satan's pride.

> For you [Satan] have said in your heart: "I will ascend into heaven, I will exalt my throne above the stars of God; I will also sit on the mount of the congregation On the farthest sides of the north; I will ascend above the heights of the clouds, I will be like the Most High."
>
> Isaiah 14:13–14

Daniel tells us the result of a king's pride.

> O king, the Most High God gave Nebuchadnezzar your father a kingdom and majesty, glory and honor. And because of the majesty that He gave him, all peoples, nations, and languages trembled and feared before him. Whomever he wished, he executed; whomever he wished, he kept alive;

whomever he wished, he set up; and whomever he wished, he put down. But when his heart was lifted up, and his spirit was hardened in pride, he was deposed from his kingly throne, and they took his glory from him. Then he was driven from the sons of men, his heart was made like the beasts, and his dwelling *was* with the wild donkeys. They fed him with grass like oxen, and his body was wet with the dew of heaven, till he knew that the Most High God rules in the kingdom of men, and appoints over it whomever He chooses.

But you his son, Belshazzar, have not humbled your heart, although you knew all this. And you have lifted yourself up against the Lord of heaven. They have brought the vessels of His house before you, and you and your lords, your wives and your concubines, have drunk wine from them. And you have praised the gods of silver and gold, bronze and iron, wood and stone, which do not see or hear or know; and the God who *holds* your breath in His hand and owns all your ways, you have not glorified.

Daniel 5:18–23

The Gospel of Mark tells us about a heart full of pride.

And He said, "What comes out of a man, that defiles a man. For from within, out of the heart of men, proceed evil thoughts, adulteries, fornications, murders, thefts, covetousness, wickedness, deceit, lewdness, an evil eye, blasphemy, pride, foolishness. All these evil things come from within and defile a man."

Mark 7:20–23

Called to Be Different

In 1 John, we read John's description of pride.

> Do not love the world or the things in the world. If anyone loves the world, the love of the Father is not in him. For all that *is* in the world—the lust of the flesh, the lust of the eyes, and the pride of life—is not of the Father but is of the world. And the world is passing away, and the lust of it; but he who does the will of God abides forever.
>
> 1 John 2:15–17

I believe this next one probably had the biggest impact on me. It is from the Gospel of Luke.

> The Pharisee stood and prayed thus with himself, "God, I thank You that I am not like other men—extortioners, unjust, adulterers, or even as this tax collector. I fast twice a week; I give tithes of all that I possess."
>
> Luke 18:11–12

Oh my! Here is the next part in Luke 18:13–14.

> And the tax collector, standing afar off, would not so much as raise *his* eyes to heaven, but beat his breast, saying, "God, be merciful to me a sinner!" I tell you, this man went down to his house justified *rather* than the other; for everyone who exalts himself will be humbled, and he who humbles himself will be exalted.
>
> Luke 18:13–14

Need I say more? I am praying and asking the Lord to continue to develop a spirit of meekness in me. I am asking him to continue to show me areas of hidden pride in my life. I am praying for the Lord's mercy on me, a sinner saved *only* through God's grace.

I believe that in the United States we are so consumed with a spirit of pride that it practically rules everything we do. I pray that we, including me, will humble ourselves before God decides that he needs to do it for us. I pray for the blinders to be lifted. I pray for eyes to see, ears to hear, and a heart that seeks change.

Part of God's "call to be different" includes walking in the Spirit, evidenced by the presence of the fruit of the Spirit in our lives. When I see Jesus and his plan for me, I can choose to let go of thoughts, feelings, and actions that are not of him. I can choose to submit to his will and purpose for my life. When we allow our focus to be on Jesus, his plan for our life here on this earth, and our eternal life yet to come, then we can more freely let go of those fleshy desires that try to hold us back.

Workplace Ministry

I shared with you how the Lord has used me at the college to pray with faculty, staff, and students. This is one of the reasons he gifts us and places us where he does; we are to be his eyes and ears in that territory. We are to be his mouthpiece, speaking words of the kingdom—comfort, blessing, forgiveness, and love—to all we meet and minister to in his name. More importantly, we are to be his hands that touch, bless, and heal. The church has slowly been awakening to this reality of *workplace ministry*. The Lord calls many of his disciples (us) to be apostles, prophets, evangelists, pastors, and teachers *within our everyday world.*

The Lord calls us to minister on our jobs. This is not just with regard to praying with our fellow workers (although that is a big part of it), but it involves being an instrument of positive change within our work environment. We are called to improve conditions in the area where he has called us to work. In my call, this has meant to improve conditions for the betterment of the health-care students whom I serve.

The Joseph Blessing

For me, these things I have mentioned represent the "Joseph blessing." Do you remember the story of Joseph from Genesis? The Lord and Joseph's father favored him, and Joseph received prophetic dreams from the Lord. This caused jealousy among his brothers, who sold him into slavery, tricking their father into believing he was dead.

Joseph became the slave of Potiphar, the captain of Pharaoh's guard in Egypt. As the Lord's favor still rested upon Joseph, he soon became the overseer of Potiphar's house. Potiphar's wife tried to seduce Joseph. When he refused, she lied and had him thrown into prison. Due to the Lord's favor, Joseph soon was appointed head over all the prisoners by the keeper of the prison. After several years, the Pharaoh had a dream that no one could interpret. It was remembered that Joseph could interpret dreams. He was brought from the prison, interpreted the Pharaoh's dream, and was appointed by the Pharaoh to be over all of Egypt, second only to the Pharaoh himself.

Joseph was seventeen when his brothers sold him into slavery and thirty when Pharaoh made him ruler, thus bringing about the fulfillment of the dreams the Lord had

Joyce A. Howard

144

given him in his youth. Joseph was favored of the Lord. No matter what his circumstances in the natural, the Lord's favor continued to exist and bless. Despite the attempts of the enemy over a thirteen-year period to keep Joseph down, his blessing (favor) blessed all those around him.

Joseph did not choose to be sold into slavery. He did not ask to be bought by Potiphar. But once he was there in Potiphar's house, he decided to do his best to serve God by serving Potiphar. Joseph did not choose to be thrown into prison. Again, once in prison, he chose to do his best to serve God by serving the people in the prison. Joseph did not ask to interpret the Pharaoh's dream, but when asked, he did what was asked of him. Joseph had a heart based on service to God, which he lived out by serving the others in his life. Because of this, God blessed him over and over again.

Testing Center for the Students

During the first couple of years that I taught at the college, I became conscious of the time that was being spent in my classroom giving exams to the students. It seemed as if the classroom time could be better spent teaching, if only there were a way to do the testing outside of class. For students, this would mean they could have more freedom in their preparation time, in the time they chose to take their exams, and a longer period of time in which to write the exams. I spoke with some colleagues about my concerns and they agreed. We decided to set up a small, out-of-class testing service for our students on a trial basis. It was well received.

Called to Be Different

Within a few years, many of the faculty from my area were involved in the testing center, with faculty from other parts of the college asking to join in. The college granted some release time in my teaching schedule to coordinate the center, plus allowed me to hire people through a grant program so that the testing center could be open full-time.

We continued to evolve. As the college prepared for a major renovation, it was decided that we would merge the testing center with the library, the open computer labs, and other activities of the college that were centered on providing services for the students. We joined together and designed a state-of-the-art facility that has not only served the needs of my students, but also the needs of thousands of students from across the campus.

Resource-Based Learning

During my first years at the college, I was asked to join a committee that dealt with learning resources for students. As we met and brainstormed together, our committee grew and changed its name, and I became its chair. We were discovering together a whole different approach to teaching. We wrote this description.

> Using experts, local agencies, print and electronic media to develop lifelong learning skills needed in educational, occupational, and personal settings. This is *not* a way of teaching; it is a way of facilitating learning. The instructor functions as the facilitator, while the emphasis in the learning environment is on information literacy. The student is the center

Joyce A. Howard

of the learning environment. The student uses the resources given to facilitate their learning.

Members of the committee began to make presentations on the local, state, and national level, sharing our vision and facilitating changes in teaching styles. We also shared the new building design the college had integrated, the one that I mentioned earlier. We were not unique in this approach; we were simply the group at our college that was making the discovery. These changes were occurring across the country and on all levels of education. These changes revolutionized our classrooms and teaching methods.

Exposure Control Manuals

During those first years at the college, I became aware of our lack of proper guidelines with regard to exposure practices and infection control. In particular, I became aware of situations where our students were left without any clear direction, training, or protection as they went through their clinical programs. Working with fellow colleagues and with the blessing of the college president, we formed a committee to deal with these issues. From this, over time, came two exposure control manuals.

The first manual was an update for faculty, staff, and all other employees of the college. The second manual was for all students entering fields of study where guidelines were necessary, especially all healthcare students. The first manual was fairly easy to write, as it was an update and simply needed to be in alignment with state and national guidelines that already existed.

147

When we began to write the student manual, we discovered there was a void in this area. There were no other such manuals that we could locate to use as our guide. We began to formulate our needs, questions to which we had no ready answers. We organized meetings involving appropriate faculty and staff of the college, appropriate personnel from our clinical sites, and the professionals that oversee MIOSHA (Michigan Occupational Safety and Health Administration) regulations for our state. As we met together, we formulated the questions that we needed the state to determine answers for. This led to interpretations being written for the exposure control laws of our state. With this additional information, we were then able to complete the second manual. The manual was, and is, used to orient our students who enter into one of the healthcare-related clinical programs. Teaching this information is one of the main goals of the course I teach at the college.

Once this second manual was written, members of the committee made presentations at local and state gatherings to disseminate the information. We made a decision as a committee that we would freely lend our manual to other colleges, in paper format or as a file attachment, however they desired. Our goal as a committee was to make certain that the healthcare students of our state were protected throughout their clinical experience.

Microbiology for Healthcare Students

I teach microbiology and infection control. The overwhelming majority of my students are entering the healthcare field. Early on, I discovered that college microbiology textbooks, lab manuals, etc., are written for students pursuing a degree in the field of microbiology, not healthcare. As a result, another faculty member and I decided to write books that were geared more directly to our students. We wrote our own lab manual and study guide. We found a textbook-CD package that most closely lined up with our healthcare approach and then modified our presentations so that it met the needs of our students.

Since that time, other faculty members have joined with us. Together, we have updated the lab manual, making it common across the course, so that all students passing through our program have a similar experience. Together, we have updated the outcomes and objectives of our course, plus developed the assessment tools used to determine the success of our students. There has been a tremendous dedication on the part of the other faculty. Each member has taken on roles of writing documents, grants, and whatever has been needed to improve the learning experience of our students.

We Are to Be a Blessing

As a born-again, spirit-filled child of God, I know that I am favored of the Lord. No matter where I go, that blessing manifests itself. My blessing has brought blessing on my job to all those around me at the college—faculty, staff, and especially students.

I did not seek to make changes happen at the college. I believe the testing center was God's idea, an idea he brought

149

into fruition by using me and the others who joined with me. The same is true for the various manuals and other texts that were written. I, along with others, saw needs, and then we acted upon those needs. I believe this is how God speaks to us and uses us in workplace ministry.

Kenneth Copeland teaches that this is the blessing of Abraham.[48] I would agree, since Joseph is Abraham's descendant. And we walk in the blessing that was spoken through Moses in Deuteronomy 28:1–14. Praise the Lord for his faithfulness and loving-kindness! Praise the Lord for his blessing and favor!

I continue to seek the Lord and commit my life to him. I continue to seek his direction for my life. He has sent me to pray for physical healing with family members, friends, neighbors, and fellow workers. He has called me to be a leader in intercession. He has called me to speak forth his message of blessing to my family. He has given me words to share with family and friends. He has used me to speak to the broken in spirit at the jail. He has opened doors for me to sit under various ministries and grow in my knowledge and faith in him. There is nothing more exciting in this world than to say yes to Jesus, to live in, walk in, and to spread his kingdom! Mark 16 records this message of Jesus:

> And He said to them, "Go into all the world and preach the gospel to every creature. He who believes and is baptized will be saved; but he who does not believe will be condemned. And these signs will follow those who believe: In My name they will cast out demons; they will speak with new tongues; they will take up serpents; and if

they drink anything deadly, it will by no means hurt them; they will lay hands on the sick, and they will recover."

So then, after the Lord had spoken to them, He was received up into heaven, and sat down at the right hand of God. And they went out and preached everywhere, the Lord working with *them* and confirming the word through the accompanying signs. Amen.

Mark 16:15–20

This is his call to each one of us. We are to heal and deliver. We are to spread the good news of his kingdom to all those around us. We are called to concretely spread his kingdom. This means we are to bring wholeness and goodness to whatever situation we are in. We are to actively work to change the conditions of the world in which we live. The world should be a better place because we were in it. When I retire from the college, it should be a better place because I worked there, because the favor of God was there with me. Not because of me, but because of God. His favor blesses, and he has chosen to work through us. We are members of the body of Christ. God has appointed us to be a blessing to the world around us, to be his eyes and ears and hands, to touch and heal and bless.

God's Call to Intercession

My Nephew Tom

On the Saturday after Thanksgiving 2006, my sister, Pat, had stopped over to visit in the afternoon. I invited her to stay and eat. As we were visiting and sharing about all the Lord had been doing in our lives, suddenly I heard the Lord's prayer signal to me. Many will feel they do not understand, and yet some of you will. It is a special signal the Lord gives to me when he calls me to deep intercessory prayer. This particular signal is unique for me and most likely would be something entirely different for others, perhaps not even involving sound.

The signal he uses for me is one I understand from

my growing-up years. In our high school, whenever the old-fashioned PA system was turned on to make an announcement, there would first be this loud, high-pitched sound. This would be followed by the person making the announcement.

When the Lord calls me to specific prayer, I hear that high-pitched sound in both my ears, and I know immediately that the Lord is calling me to prayer. I do not necessarily know in that instant what it is I am being called to pray for, just that I am being called to pray. Not knowing, I begin to intercede in the Spirit. I pray as I am led in my prayer language. And as I sense specific things the Lord is asking me to pray, I speak them out.

On this occasion, as Pat and I prayed together, I was led first to bind the spirit of death. I did this immediately and with all the force and authority that the Lord gave to me. After I did this, I then spoke life into the situation in Jesus' name.

Next, the Lord led me to bind the spirit of suicide. He showed me how this spirit of suicide comes to people who are in life-or-death situations and coaxes them into choosing death by giving up on life. It says to the person things such as, "No one will care if you choose not to go on," "Who will miss you anyway," "You know that no one really cares," "Life will go on," "It won't hurt anyone if you just let go."

The spirit of suicide feeds these lies to the person at his or her weakest and most defenseless point. That is how evil and despicable the enemy is. I believe that Jesus allowed me to see how this spirit works so that I could help others to recognize and stand up against it.

From that time of intercession with my sister, which was very powerful and went on for quite some time, those are the main points that I remember. Perhaps my sister would remember more things. In fact, I am certain she would, as the Spirit is also teaching and guiding her. The Lord had brought her there (totally unplanned by either of us, but by the Lord) to both be a witness to and take part in this intercession for my nephew, Tom. He is my nephew through my husband's family. He suffered a road bike accident that crushed T5, the fifth thoracic vertebra of his spinal column.[49]

Of course, I did not know that was whom the intercession was for. At the time, I thought about my nephew, as I knew he was struggling deeply with his grandmother's death the Sunday before. But I thought of others too that I knew were in struggles. The Lord did not reveal to me that I was specifically praying for him. And this is how it commonly is when he calls me to deep intercession.

You see, it really does not matter whom it is I am called to intercede for. It does not matter if I know the person or not. It does not matter what the particulars are. What matters are my willingness and my obedience. It matters to the Lord that I am obedient, that he knows he can call on me whenever there is a need. And that when he does, I will understand and will not ignore the call, the sense, the awareness, the feeling, whatever means he uses to call me. The Lord is looking for such people. Perhaps the Lord is looking for you.

It took quite a while after this happened for my spirit and emotions to quiet back down. My sister and I continued our visit, ate our lunch, and prayed together again before she left. However, the depth of feeling and emotion that was aroused inside of me was hard to set aside. It was hard to just calm down and proceed in a normal fashion.

Those of you who have experienced this know what I am talking about. You have stood before the Holy of holies. Your petition was not just words you were saying, but your whole being was somehow involved in the giving of the petition.

The next morning I received a call telling me about my nephew's accident and that he was in the hospital. As soon as I could get myself ready, I headed across the state. I knew that I needed to go over and pray over him with his family, anointing him for protection and healing. I knew how loved and precious he was to the Lord. I knew that the Lord did not just want him to survive; the Lord wanted him to be physically and spiritually raised up.

The Lord would use what the enemy meant for evil to bring his good and to bring his glory. The Lord would use this time and this accident to bring a powerful witness to my nephew and to all his family and friends. It would not happen instantaneously, but over time, the Lord would use this incident to bring many to him. He would use it to bring many who love him and who have been raised up in religious traditions, to reach beyond that and seek him. To discover for the first time, or rediscover, a truth lost— the person of Jesus. To recognize that the Lord's call has always been to him, to a personal relationship with him. Not to a ritual or a tradition or a tale, but to the reality of the risen Lord, Jesus Christ.

Praise God for the blessing of cell phones in our day.

All along the trip across the state, I was able to call my fellow intercessors to join me in prayer. I was thankful for each one that I had programmed into my cell phone and that the Lord allowed me to reach. They were a great comfort along the journey. Each stepped right in and began powerful intercession on the Lord's behalf. Each allowed themselves to be open for the Lord's direction on how to pray. And each accepted the authority and power the Lord had given to them to intercede on the behalf of others. For we do not pray in our own power and authority, but in that given to us by the Lord Jesus Christ. We must recognize and accept that this power is there, freely given by the Lord so that we can intercede for one another.

When I arrived in the hospital room, his parents and his girlfriend were there. I had taken my anointing oil with me. I knew in my heart and mind that I was going to need to be able to pray freely in the Spirit, so I explained this and asked their permission. They agreed. I then asked them to join me in laying hands and anointing him. We did that. I started us out, praying both in English and in the Spirit for all that the Lord wanted done in his life. His parents and girlfriend each took a turn adding prayers, using the oil to make the sign of the cross on his forehead, and laying hands on him for healing.

Nothing magical happened, as the Lord is not into magic. But something changed in the spirit; *in the unseen world of God's kingdom, God's will was done.*

Within my husband's family, we believe in God, and we believe in Jesus, in his will and right to heal. What often falls short in our belief is that the Lord wants to heal us concretely, physically, in the *now*. My husband's brother, Mark (Tom's father), has come to fully believe in this reality. In fact, the Lord has begun to use him in a healing ministry. I believe it will become a reality to his wife that she too is a part of this call and plan. Praise God! Praise him for his love and generosity and favor!

On my way back home that day, the Lord spoke into my spirit a word for his parents. I was to call them and let them know that two reports were going to come to them concerning their son, and only one of those reports would be the Lord's. A bad report was going to come forth, and they were *not* to accept it; when this report came forth, they were *not* to put any belief in it. It was very important that they *not* listen to this report or put any trust in it because if they did, they would cause that report to become a reality.

I wonder how often this happens. I wonder how often our acceptance of the enemy's word (report) causes it to become a reality in our life. Just the thought of this puts the fear of the Lord in me. Now, when I say "fear of the Lord," I do not mean that I am frightened. I am speaking of a deep reverence and respect for the almighty Lord of this universe. Lord Jesus, help us to draw closer to you and only listen for your words. Help us to discern your words. Help us to recognize your reports.

After my nephew's surgery, the initial word was positive. Later that evening, a very negative report came forth. The report was that he had negative pressure pulmonary edema and was on a respirator. His mother, Diane, and his girlfriend (who is now his wife), Bethany, were there at the time the report was given. Diane recognized immediately that this was the bad report they were not to accept. By the next day, they were able to remove him from the respirator.

Within a week of his arrival at the hospital, Tom was ready to go home. He had to rest appropriately for a period of time and wear a brace at certain times. But the biggest warning that he was given was to not overdo it. His biggest challenge was to be patient with the healing process. Praise God! That's not a bad place to be!

At the time, I prayed that Tom's physical healing would also be a time of spiritual and emotional (inner) healing for him. God wants to heal us spirit, soul, and body. What the Lord wants most of all is a spiritual awakening, or reawakening, for all of us.

Further Calls to Intercession

I want to share with you now some further incidences where the Lord has specifically called me to deep intercessory prayer. I believe the Lord is asking me to share them to help many of you to have faith in the Lord's call to you in intercessory prayer.

A different but similar experience of intercession occurred for me Labor Day weekend of 2005.[50] It was less than two months after my husband had gone on to his glory in heaven. It involved our niece, Anna, on my husband's side of our family. My husband and I had always felt especially close to this niece. Of course, at the time of the incident, I did not realize that it was her that the Lord was calling me to pray for.

On this particular day, I just happened to be walking

into my husband's old bedroom. Suddenly I felt my body literally being picked up into the air and thrown a distance across the room. When I hit the floor, I was in deep intercession, the deepest kind, which involves wailing in the spirit. I did not know exactly what had happened or whom it was I was praying for, but I knew it involved the death of someone and was very traumatic. I knew it involved some member of our family.

I began praying in the Spirit and sobbing in the natural. As the Lord led me, I began to intercede. What I felt was that I was comforting someone who was experiencing a death he could not stop and that was shaking him to the core of his being. My main goal seemed to be that I pray God's comfort to this person, that the Lord give him the ability to withstand this overwhelming pain he was experiencing.

I do not know how long I prayed. As I was wailing, sobbing, and praying as best I could, time lost meaning. I kept it up until I felt the burden lift. And even then it was impossible to just go back to things normal. I sat on the couch and cried and cried, trying to comfort myself. I had no idea who this had happened to. The only thing I knew was that it was someone very close to me. I didn't know if it was one of my children or grandchildren, one of my sisters or a member of their families, or someone from my husband's side of our family. Part of me wanted to get on the phone and try to verify where everyone was and if everyone was okay. I knew that was not really practical and probably impossible. I felt that same urge and helplessness on September 11, 2001, when the twin towers fell. I am sure you know what I mean.

The next day the call came about our niece. While biking in a park with her husband, Roman, and her stepson, David, a driver hit her full force and knocked her up against a concrete embankment. Despite the fact she was wearing protective gear, the impact killed her instantly. She died right there in Roman's arms. It was for him I was called to pray.

Another experience of this level of intercession occurred while driving home from a professional meeting that had occurred downstate on a university campus.[51] I was alone in the car and had just gotten out of the heavier city traffic. I saw an accident occurring in the other lane of the expressway. I did not see how it got started, but I watched a car being turned around and hit from various directions. In my rearview mirror, I could see all the southbound traffic coming to a standstill. I immediately began to intercede in the Spirit for everyone involved in the accident.

Suddenly I went into deep intercession, wailing, sobbing, and crying out to the Lord on behalf of a specific person. It was the mother who was in the backseat of the car with her daughter, who was literally dying in her arms. I could see it all in my mind as clearly as if I was there in the car with them. I can still see it now. I was interceding for the life of this little girl. I was crying out loudly and telling the Lord that he could not allow this little child to die in her mother's arms. I was reminding the Lord of all the plans he had for this little girl and that this was not his will or plan for her life.

The intensity of the intercession was so great that I literally had to pull to the side of the expressway. I was sobbing and moaning so deeply that I could not keep driving the car, nor was it safe for me to be doing so. I would pray until I thought I was going to be okay and then pull back on the expressway, only to get a few miles and be so deep in intercession that I again had to pull off the expressway. This kept up all the way back home. It took me hours to make a trip that would normally have been maybe an hour's journey. I was absolutely exhausted and depleted of all energy when I got home.

I never met these people, and they never knew I spent this time in intercession for them. But I do know through the Spirit that the little girl survived. Praise God! When the Lord calls us to intercession for others, it is not about us. It is about a tremendous need the Lord sees, and he needs human beings on the earth willing to intercede for this need. That is how important our prayers are to God. Our prayers rise as incense to the throne of God.

Does God need us to respond? Yes! Could he sovereignly intervene if he wanted to? Yes! But he gave this world to mankind. He prefers to work through us. *The Lord is looking throughout the earth for those he can call on to pray.* He is asking us to become sensitive and in tune to his call. He is asking us to let go of our doubt and unbelief and pride, listening and responding to his call.

So I want you to know that we have a choice in how we respond to the Lord in intercession. He will not violate our free will, nor will he do things out of order. Just as is true in every other aspect of our walk with the Lord, we have a choice in how we respond to his call for intercessory prayer. I pray that each of us will be strong in our faith. I pray that we will listen faithfully for his call (his signal) and respond fully. I pray we will set aside pride and doubt to respond.

God will not only use different methods to call us to intercession, but he will call us to different degrees of intercession. I have shared with you what have been the most powerful experiences, as I have discovered that many people are afraid to share such experiences for fear of not being believed.

God has called me many times to intercession by simply placing a burden on my heart for a particular person. Another way he has called me is that I will keep seeing a particular person's face in the faces of people I meet on the street or see on the television until it finally hits me that I keep seeing this person's face because God wants me to pray for him or her. Another way God calls me to intercession is by continually bringing thoughts and memories of a particular person to mind. Sometimes I will catch on right away (that it is God, and he wants me to pray), and other times the Lord has to keep giving me hints until I finally respond.

The most obvious ways God calls me to intercession is by the person calling to ask for prayer or someone else calling to ask me to pray for the person, alerting me to the need. God has no shortage of ways to call us to intercession. You do not have to be afraid of where or how the Lord will lead you, simply trust in him to give you what you are ready for. God will never give us more than we are ready and able to handle.

Jesus Taught Us to Pray

The Lord wants each of you to know how unique and special you are to him. Each of you brings a blessing that only you can bring. You have a special way of praying that no one else has. You have an authority when you pray, a confidence and boldness that the Lord has given you. It is a blessing to the Lord.

Jesus himself listens to each of you when you pray. Please let this truth sink in: Jesus pricks up his ears and turns his whole attention to you when you pray. Jesus loves to hear you pray. It thrills him to hear you. He listens for your honesty and sincerity. He longs for your wholeness and integrity and desire to live for him. He desires for you to value family above all else. Praise God! Is that exciting or what?

God is your Father. The Creator of the heavens and the earth wants you to call him daddy. He longs for your excitement and determination. He desires that you look for him and to him in every situation. Father God loves coming down to walk and talk with you. That is so special to him. He used to love to do that with Adam. It is a favorite activity, and he is so pleased when you love doing it with him.

No unworthiness. Rebuke any attempt of the enemy to make you feel "less than," no matter what happens. To such a thought, say, "equal to" or "better than." Say, "I can do all things through Christ who strengthens me" (Philippians 4:13). Cast off any thoughts of inferiority. They are not from your Father. They are not from your Savior. Put an end to such thoughts once and for all. Speak forth your victory.

Do not allow one single doubt about the goodness of God. If God made you, which he did, then you are a holy, worthy vessel. You are the temple of the Holy Spirit. God himself dwells in you. Decree it. Stand on it. Hold your ground. Do not give up an inch. Psalm 121 is for you.

> I will lift up my eyes to the hills—From whence comes my help? My help comes from the LORD, Who made heaven and earth. He will not allow your foot to be moved; He who keeps you will not slumber. Behold, He who keeps Israel Shall neither slumber nor sleep. The LORD is your keeper; The LORD is your shade at your right hand. The sun shall not strike you by day, Nor the moon by night.
>
> The LORD shall preserve you from all evil; He shall preserve your soul. The LORD shall preserve

your going out and your coming in From this time forth, and even forevermore.

Psalm 121:1–8

Jesus taught his disciples how to pray, which we call the Lord's Prayer. The Gospel of Matthew records these words of Jesus.

In this manner, therefore, pray: Our Father in heaven, Hallowed be Your name. Your kingdom come. Your will be done On earth as *it is* in heaven. Give us this day our daily bread. And forgive us our debts, As we forgive our debtors. And do not lead us into temptation, But deliver us from the evil one. For Yours is the kingdom and the power and the glory forever. Amen.

Matthew 6:9–13

Each time we pray this prayer, we are recognizing the sovereignty of God as the Creator of the heavens and the earth. We are recognizing his position in our lives as our Father, and we are glorifying him. We are acknowledging our belief in the existence of heaven and that God's will is done there. We are then praying for God's kingdom, the only message Jesus preached, to come here on earth. And as a result of that coming, for God's will to be done here on earth, the same as it is in heaven.

Each time we pray this prayer, we are asking our Father God to meet our daily needs, all of them, whatever they may be. We are asking our Father to forgive us for any way we have sinned and blocked his desire to bless us here on this earth. We pray contingent upon the fact that we acknowledge and forgive anyone who has sinned against us.

Each time we pray this prayer, we are asking our Father God to keep us from temptation. For him to do this, we must listen to that inner voice of the Spirit of God, which attempts to guide us; keeping us from harm, strife, bitterness, unhappiness, and activities that would move us away from God's will for our lives.

I researched at least a dozen different Bible translations. In verse thirteen, all but two versions called him "the evil one." One translation simply called him "the devil." One translation said "deliver us from evil." I think the consensus among Bible translators was that Jesus was referring to Satan here. Each time we pray the Lord's Prayer, we are praying to be forgiven of our sins, to be kept from temptations, and to be delivered from Satan.

Jesus Preached the Kingdom of God

Jesus taught his disciples and followers about the kingdom of God. Immediately after being baptized by John the Baptist, scripture tells us, "From that time Jesus began to preach and to say, 'Repent, for the kingdom of heaven is at hand'" (Matthew 4:17). This passage in Matthew continues and tells us what Jesus preached about the kingdom: "And Jesus went about all Galilee, teaching in their synagogues, preaching the gospel of the kingdom, and healing all kinds of sickness and all kinds of disease among the people" (Matthew 4:23).

In fact, Matthew gives fifty direct quotes from Jesus

where he is preaching about the kingdom of God having arrived on our earth. Luke gives thirty-seven direct quotes from Jesus preaching the kingdom, whereas Mark gives sixteen, and John gives five. Please read through the gospels again to see exactly what Jesus said and taught. He had no other message apart from the fulfillment of God's kingdom here on this earth.

Remember again that in the Lord's Prayer—given to us by Jesus—we are taught to acknowledge that heaven is God's kingdom, and we are then exhorted to pray for that kingdom with its dominion, rule, and blessings to be fulfilled here on our earth. We are not so much asking for it to come in the sense that it is not here yet as we are asking for its fulfillment to exist in our daily lives so that we will live and walk knowing that we are in his kingdom and that we will minister to others out of his kingdom.

Jesus Wants Us to Be in Full Health

Many of you have been blessed through your struggles and trials, and I would absolutely agree. God promises that if we follow him, he will work everything to our good. God is not the author of sickness or disease. We know instinctively as parents that we do not want our children to be sick. When they are, we do everything in our power to help them to get well, including praying to the Lord to heal them. Each of us takes advantage of doctors and medicine because we know that their purpose is in alignment with the Lord's—that we be well.

But when do we usually pray and ask for healing? I

believe that in America, we have gotten out of alignment (order). We have been taught to run to the doctor for any and every thing that occurs, and we expect the doctor to give us at least one kind of medicine even if we really do not need it. Then and only then, if the doctor and medicine do not solve the problem, we begin to pray. Now, I know this is not true for some of you; I know some of you turn to the Lord right away, the first thing, and ask for the Lord's healing. But going to the doctor or the emergency clinic or the emergency room of the hospital has become so commonplace in our society that we often forget about the Lord. We do not consider the fact that God heals, that Jesus came to restore the gift of healing. In fact, we forget that Jesus wants us to be in full health, that it is part of God's will for our daily lives and something we are to pray and have faith for every single day.

When a family member is sick, we suffer with them. Family and friends do everything they can to help. Ted and I would never have made it through the years we struggled with his MS without the help, love, support, and prayers of family and friends. But if any of our family members or friends could have come sooner in Jesus' name to heal him of the MS, neither of us would have hesitated to accept it.

Healing, wholeness, and wellness are God's design, desire, and destiny for each of us. The whole pattern of Jesus' life, his words and actions, was about restoration and bringing the kingdom of God to the earth as it is right now in heaven. Jesus never told a single person he came across that he was going to leave them sick or in bondage, because he knew they would grow as an individual through the process.

I absolutely agree that we grow through our trials. But perhaps the biggest struggle we are facing is separating out in our present-day, secular-driven worlds which trials are from God and which trials are from Satan. That in itself is a momentous task given this world we live in, where God and prayer are increasingly banned from our schools, government, courts, etc. If we truly believed that sickness made us stronger as individuals, we would never go to a doctor or take medicine again. *Trials don't make you strong; it is your reaction to the trials that makes you strong.* It is what Jesus did with the temptations he faced that made him strong. We are asked to do the same. When we do, we show our true character and the character of the Lord who is in us.

A family member once asked about a child who was severely impaired. They asked if her impairment represented a curse or a punishment for sin committed by some past generation. I responded that I did not believe it was God's perfect will for us to go through such struggles, but God has chosen not to override the free will of man. He gave this world to man. Jesus died so that all could be healed and born whole. And yet, the total fulfillment of that has not yet come.

God in his mercy gave this child to loving parents, knowing their tremendous love, understanding, and compassion would bless this child, even as she blessed them. Many children born severely impaired are discarded right from birth. In most countries they are literally thrown out. If possible, they are aborted before they can be born. And yet, whole families have been blessed because of their relationship with such a child. That is God's mercy and grace at its very best. Only God can take a seemingly hopeless situation and bring goodness from it.

Having said all that, I again say that Jesus wants healing, wholeness, and deliverance for all. He gave his life to bring this about. That is what Jesus would choose, especially for a severely impaired child. I pray that we all grow together in the grace of God. My desire is that we be freed from any hindrances that are holding us back from this growth. My desire is that no child or grandchild be born suffering from MS, diabetes, or any other disease or affliction.

Jesus Desires a Personal Relationship with Us

Jesus desires a close, personal relationship with me. He speaks to me about issues in my life that are separating me from him. He will do the same with you. These are the things the Lord has been speaking to me to put down: doubt, unbelief, bitterness, unforgiveness, pride, and manipulation (which is a form of witchcraft).

I believe the Lord has a specific word for your bruised and callused heart. He says that as his Word is built precept upon precept, your heart has been hardened hurt upon hurt. The Lord wants to heal that. I decree wholeness within you—spirit, soul, and body. This is the season in which you will see the Lord's miracle-working power. Together, he has placed his anointing upon us. Together, we are to speak forth healing and wholeness. This is the season. This is our time in him. We are to speak it forth in fullness of faith, with no cloud of doubt or unbelief, with no unforgiveness or bitterness. We must pray and repent as the Lord leads us to make it so.

Jesus and the Word Are One

Jesus and the Word are one. We cannot know Jesus without knowing the Word. "In the beginning was the Word, and the Word was with God, and the Word was God" (John 1:1). Jesus is the embodiment of the Word made flesh, a human being like us, so that we can feel and touch and know God through Jesus in the same way we know another human being. "And the Word became flesh and dwelt among us, and we beheld His glory, the glory as of the only begotten of the Father, full of grace and truth" (John 1:14).

God tells us how important his Word is to our well-being. His Word brings us true life and health. We hear these words in Proverbs:

> My son, give attention to my words; Incline your ear to my sayings. Do not let them depart from your eyes; Keep them in the midst of your heart; For they *are* life to those who find them, And health to all their flesh. Keep your heart with all diligence, For out of it *spring* the issues of life.
>
> Proverbs 4:20–23

God calls us to know his Word. He will bless us as we meditate upon and live by his Word.

"If you diligently heed the voice of the Lord your God and do what is right in His sight, give ear to His commandments and keep all His statutes, I will put none of the diseases on you which I have brought on the Egyptians. For I *am* the Lord who heals you."

Exodus 15:26

The Word of God is our primary weapon against the powers of darkness that try to come against us here on the earth. It is part of the armor we are exhorted to put on every day so that we can live a victorious life.

Jesus resisted Satan's temptations by quoting the Word of God to him. In his gospel, Matthew tells us Jesus' response to Satan:

> But He answered and said, "It is written, *'Man shall not live by bread alone, but by every word that proceeds from the mouth of God.'"*

Matthew 4:4

Again and again as he was tempted, Jesus responded by saying, "It is written..."[52] This must be our response when the enemy tries to tempt us or to attack us with sickness or financial hardship. This can only happen when we learn his Word; get it down deep into our hearts and minds through study, meditation, memorization, and by the Holy Spirit's revelation. Jesus wants us to speak and pray the Word back to him and to our Father.

The Believer's Authority

Authority is a privilege given by God. It originates with and comes from God. The Greek word for authority is *exousia*. To operate in authority requires grace, the empowering ability through God to do what you cannot do in your own strength. Grace raises you to the standard to do that which truth demands of you.

The purpose of our authority is service to the people of God through the power of the Holy Spirit. Service requires humility and submission. True humility is believing what God says. We must be submitted to the Word as Jesus was submitted to the Word. We must know who we are in Christ. The basis for our authority is Jesus, his resurrection and exaltation by his Father. God's love is

Called to Be Different

175

the key component to operating effectively in authority. Perfect love casts out all fear. Integrating God's love into our lives demonstrates that we are abiding in him. Jesus must be our example in all things. He only did and said what he saw the Father do and say. Likewise, we are commanded to only do and say what we see Jesus do and say.

Authority is delegated; it is by God's design and for his purpose. Authority operates in faith, trust, and submission. You cannot be a person with authority unless you are a person under authority. The authority of the believer is revealed more fully in the book of Ephesians than any other Epistle. We need to put on the whole armor of God in order to operate effectively in God-given authority.

The Whole Armor of God

Ephesians chapter six states:

> Finally, my brethren, be strong in the Lord and in the power of His might. Put on the whole armor of God, that you may be able to stand against the wiles of the devil. For we do not wrestle against flesh and blood, but against principalities, against powers, against the rulers of the darkness of this age, against spiritual *hosts* of wickedness in the heavenly *places*. Therefore take up the whole armor of God, that you may be able to withstand in the evil day, and having done all, to stand. Stand therefore, having girded your waist with truth, having put on the breastplate of righteousness, and having shod your feet with the preparation of the gospel of peace; above all, taking the shield of faith with which you will be able to

Joyce A. Howard

quench all the fiery darts of the wicked one. And take the helmet of salvation, and the sword of the Spirit, which is the word of God; praying always with all prayer and supplication in the Spirit, being watchful to this end with all perseverance and supplication for all the saints.

Ephesians 6:10–18

I am going to illustrate Ephesians 6:10–18 as a teaching and go through its points.

> "Finally, my brethren, be strong in the Lord and in the power of his might…"

First, we are told to look to the Lord, to be strong in him and in the power of his might. The joy of the Lord is our strength. We are to rejoice, and again I say rejoice. Scripture tells us that he who waits on the Lord shall renew his strength; he shall mount up as eagles.

God's blessings are for those who abide in the presence of the Almighty. We are told that we shall receive power when the Holy Spirit has come upon us. When we abide in the Word and let the Word abide in us, we will become stronger. *The enemy's number-one tactic is to take the Word from us because it is our source of power.* Do not let the enemy pull you away from God's Word. Stay strong in his Word. Read the Word every day. Meditate upon it. Study it. Let the Word be your guide for all decisions concerning your life.

> "Put on the whole armor of God…"

Next, we are told that we need the whole armor. In fact, Paul mentions this fact twice. We need to be prepared *in advance* of an attack; there is not time during an attack to get prepared. We are to be like a nation's "standing army," standing ready at all times for battle.

The armor is put on from the inside out, not the outside in. Jesus needs to clean us up first. The way we *put on* Christ is to immerse ourselves in the ways that Jesus thinks and behaves. Christian soldiers and warriors must display self-denial, courage, and endurance.

> "...that you may be able to stand against the wiles of the devil..."

The wiles of the devil are his schemes, plans, attacks, and strategies. He is organized; attacks are planned, not random. I discovered that God's Word needed to be secure in both my mind and my heart so that when a battle came (sickness, words spoken contrary to God's Word, or other attacks), I was ready and able to respond.

I have mentioned that the two main attacks on me as a child (and throughout much of my life) have been rejection and sexual sin.

I have mentioned that two of Satan's attacks on Ted and me included disease and poverty. There were others, but these were some of the main ones we had to fight.

Early in my Christian walk, I needed other believers to help me do this. In fact, we always need the help of other faith believers. They bolster us and help us to stand secure.

"For we do not wrestle against flesh and blood, but against principalities, against powers, against the rulers of the darkness of this age, against spiritual hosts of wickedness in the heavenly places."

We are told that since the battle is spiritual, our weapons must be spiritual. The number-one battleground is within our minds. Satan is trying to build strongholds and fortresses in our minds. Strongholds of the mind oppose the truth of the Gospel and the truth of the Word of God.

Stronghold is defined as a place where a particular group, activity, or set of opinions is concentrated.[53] According to Pastor Barbara Yoder, a stronghold is a "house of thoughts."[54] Strongholds include doubt, unbelief, prejudices, and preconceptions. Strongholds lead to bigotry. Bigotry involves holding strong opinions, especially in politics, religion, or ethnicity, and refusing to accept different views.[55] Bigots refuse to accept other views, especially God's Word on a matter.

Demonic strongholds blind men's minds. Only spiritual weapons can penetrate and break down strongholds of the mind. I discovered that there were many strongholds (thought patterns) that were holding my mind in bondage against God's Word. As you open yourself up more and more to the Lord, you too will discover these weights. Let them be dislodged from your mind. Let the Lord Jesus and his Spirit set you free. Our thoughts should always agree with God's Word.

Paul describes our weapons as part of our armor. Read on to learn more about how you can break the strongholds

Called to Be Different

that are holding your mind in doubt, unbelief, prejudice, and preconception by making use of your armor.

We wrestle against principalities and powers of the enemy. Wrestling is the most intense form of conflict. It requires every part of your mind and body and every skill.

Satan's kingdom is comprised of various areas and levels of authority (principalities and powers). He rules from the second heaven, which is an area between heaven and earth. Satan is referred to in Scripture as "the prince of the power of the air" (Ephesians 2:2b).

"Therefore take up the whole armor of God..."

We must take up the whole armor of God if we are to withstand and prevail. It requires obedience. Soldiers submit to their superiors. It can only be done through faith and love. To withstand means to vigorously oppose, bravely resist, stand your ground, or stand face-to-face against the adversary.

We need to put on the whole armor; no partial equipment will suffice. Jesus provides us with the armor, and the Holy Spirit makes it ours. We put it on as we claim it verbally by faith. Satan never quits. We have to fight through to the end. We must withstand and then stand. We gain, hold, and then advance. We stand *ready* for the fight, and we stand *in* the fight.

The Apostle Paul (who wrote the book of Ephesians) specifically mentions six pieces of our armor: our belt, breastplate, boots, shield, helmet, and sword. These are the pieces of armor that any soldier would be concerned about and take care with to make sure they were secured.

> "Stand therefore, having girded your waist with truth…"

The first part of our armor is truth. We are to wear truth as a belt strapped around our waists. Truth is higher than fact. Truth requires us to put away hypocrisy, sham, religious clichés, empiricism, etc.

Hypocrisy is defined as the false claim to or pretense of having admirable principles, beliefs, or feelings.[56] A *hypocrite* is a person who pretends to have these admirable principles, beliefs, or feelings but behaves otherwise.[57] We must be willing to do what we say. If our actions do not match our words, we are hypocrites, and we are not walking in the truth.

This was part of the reality I discovered about myself in March of 2005 when Kaye came to pray with us for Ted's healing. I discovered there was much bitterness and resentment in me for things that had happened over the years. I had to get right with God about those things. I had to forgive wrongs that were done to me, even by my closest family and friends. When we do not forgive others, that is hypocrisy, and it holds back the truth of God's Word from being able to work in our lives. When we do not forgive, it is like a cloud that hides the truth of Jesus' life and love from us. The Word says that if we do not forgive from the heart, neither will our Father forgive us, and this blocks our prayers from being answered.

Called to Be Different

I also had to look deeply at my life and face up to sins that were there that I had been glossing over. I had to confess those sins to the Lord. As long as I left them hidden, continuing to deny their existence, they were holding me in bondage. Freedom came through facing those sins, confessing them to the Lord, and allowing him to set me free. And then I had to walk in that freedom, refusing to sin anymore.

Each of us has areas within our lives we have not yet given to the Lord. I was saved by the Lord on February 26, 1976. And yet it was in March of 2005 when I was finally able to let go of things that were keeping me bound in the chains of sin. God is so patient and faithful; his love is filled with mercy and grace.

Empiricism is the philosophical belief that all knowledge is derived from the experience of the senses.[58] An empiricist believes he has to see it, hear it, touch it, smell it, or taste it for something to be real. This is living in the natural. In 1 Corinthians we are told, "But the natural man does not receive the things of the Spirit of God, for they are foolishness to him; nor can he know *them,* because they are spiritually discerned" (1 Corinthians 2:14).

From empiricism we derive expressions such as "seeing is believing." In truth, all knowledge is derived from God. Everything we see, hear, touch, smell, and taste was created by God. Everything in our universe came into existence through God's spoken word, his *rhema* word.

The fundamental laws of science, known as the laws of thermodynamics, declare energy *can* be changed from one form to another, but energy *cannot* be created or destroyed. Even scientists acknowledge that the total

Joyce A. Howard

amount of energy and matter in the universe remains constant, merely changing from one form to another.

Most countries of the world (America being the major holdout) have converted to the metric system for measurement.[59] In the metric system, water at 4°C holds the following approximate values: 1 gram of water equals 1 milliliter (ml) of water equals 1 cubic centimeter (also known as 1 cc). This allows for easy conversion between mass, volume, and length. Imagine that! And what is the main substance of our universe but water. It is considered essential for the survival of all known life. Amazing! When you study the metric system and its history, it becomes apparent that we have simply tapped into a truth of our universe. This truth allows doctors and nurses to formulate and dispense medications with accuracy.

It is only when we begin to perceive ourselves as bigger, better, or smarter than God (or we deny that God exists) that we develop empiricist thinking. The Apostle Paul said we are to gird ourselves with truth. Gird means to put a girdle or belt around yourself, to secure something to yourself with a belt, straps, or a girdle, to surround or encompass, or to prepare yourself for conflict or vigorous activity.[60] To gird up is to strengthen ourselves with the Word of God. It is imperative that we as believers have girded ourselves with God's truth so that we will not be misled by the doctrines and notions of man. We are girding ourselves so as to be strengthened in our movements. I have spoken to you already about your need to be rooted in God's Word and to stay rooted in God's Word. Jesus

Called to Be Different

described himself as "the way, the truth and the life" (John 14:6). We find our way by following Jesus.

So what is the truth of God's Word? Where does God stand on sickness versus health? Jesus is our example of the Father; he only did and said what he saw and heard the Father doing. And Jesus went about doing good and healing all he met of their diseases. So the truth about our physical bodies is that we are to walk in total health; God never ordained for us to be ill. He never ordained for Ted to suffer from MS. He never ordained for people to suffer from high blood pressure, diabetes, arthritis, migraine headaches, etc. What would happen if we truly girded ourselves in that truth?

To walk in truth requires a balance between the Word and the Spirit. We must walk in the truth, as revealed by the Lord in his Word and by the leading of the Holy Spirit, who will not direct us contrary to God's Word.

Walking in truth also has a practical application. We can no longer lie, "fudge" the truth, tell half-truths, or in any way alter or stretch the truth concerning a matter. We can no longer use the excuse that we are doing this to spare someone from hearing the truth. This is a choice and a tough decision. Our society encourages us to bend the truth. Satan knows that as long as he can keep getting us to fudge, bend, and alter the truth, he has an open doorway into our lives. You must shut that door. I must shut that door. No one can do it for us; with God's help, we must do it.

"...having put on the breastplate of righteousness..."

Paul next exhorts us to put on the breastplate of righteousness. A breastplate is worn over the chest so as to protect the heart. Righteousness is the righteousness of Christ, faith in Christ as our Savior. It is not righteousness that we can earn, for "our righteousnesses are like filthy rags" (Isaiah 64:6b). The book of Romans tells us:

> For as by one man's disobedience many were made sinners, so also by one Man's obedience many will be made righteous.
>
> Moreover the law entered that the offense might abound. But where sin abounded, grace abounded much more, so that as sin reigned in death, even so grace might reign through righteousness to eternal life through Jesus Christ our Lord.
>
> Romans 5:19–21

We were born sinners because of Adam, but we are justified and made righteous through faith in and the confession of Jesus as our Savior and Lord.

Add to this the notion that soldiers not only put on their armor, but they also train. They grow in their ability to defend themselves. As we grow in our walk with the Lord, others will experience that positive growth. First Thessalonians 5:8 describes the breastplate of faith and love as "faith working through love." In 2 Corinthians, Paul tells us, "We use the weapons of righteousness in the right hand for attack and the left hand for defense" (2 Corinthians 6:7b, NLT). Roman soldiers carried a sword in the right hand for attack, and a shield in the left for defense. Paul is telling us that our righteousness through

Christ is used for attack and that living a life of integrity is used for defense. As we walk with the Lord, we will be growing in our love walk. Our faith is shown in practical terms to others through our love for them.

First Corinthians 13:4–8 contains a description of the love that never fails:

> Love suffers long *and* is kind; love does not envy; love does not parade itself, is not puffed up; does not behave rudely, does not seek its own, is not provoked, thinks no evil; does not rejoice in iniquity, but rejoices in the truth; bears all things, believes all things, hopes all things, endures all things.
>
> Love never fails. But whether *there are* prophecies, they will fail; whether *there are* tongues, they will cease; whether *there is* knowledge, it will vanish away.
>
> 1 Corinthians 13:4–8

God's love is the substance that strengthens our breastplate. So if you say that you love your spouse (or child or friend), test it by this scripture. When he or she speaks down to you, do you suffer long and remain kind? Or do you allow the person to push all your buttons (i.e., be easily provoked)? Do you want to be proven right in all things, rejoicing when that happens (you are right) and the other person is put down?

> "…and having shod your feet with the preparation of the gospel of peace…"

Next in our armor is what covers our feet. Shoes deal with availability and mobility. We are to be always ready to carry the gospel to the lost. We need to always have our shoes on and be ready to go. Preparation, or readiness, is done in advance. We must study the Scriptures. We must understand their meaning. We must memorize the Scriptures. That is what it means to be prepared. The gospel is the good news of salvation through Jesus.

Peace means reconciliation with God—forgiveness and righteousness through faith in Jesus. We have a responsibility as believers to be prepared to share God's message of salvation, to lead others to belief in Christ. We must be ready to help someone who may be caught up in sin or iniquity (the consequences of sin) and help to set him or her free. We must be ready to pray for others to meet their needs. When the Lord's call comes, in whatever form, we must be ready to respond.

> "…above all, taking the shield of faith with which you will be able to quench all the fiery darts of the wicked one…"

We are told that, above all, we need the shield of faith. Faith is conviction, confidence, and reliance on God and what he says. It includes trust, belief, and assurance, an inward confidence. We are kept by God's power through faith. Faith deflects the fiery darts of the enemy that are directed at our heads and hearts and quenches them. Fiery darts are meant to burn us out. They can be personal attacks or corporate attacks. If you are feeling burned out,

Called to Be Different

187

what fiery dart has gotten past your shield? What can be done to put it out and to re-fire?

Each one of us falls down at some point because we are human. Each one of us needs a community of faith, a believing group of friends and a believing church, to bolster us during our moments of weakness. We must be submitted to a body of believers; otherwise, we will not have the humility to ask for help or accept the help when it is offered.

The Word of God is clear that Jesus is the head of his body, which is the church, and that his church is to be in unity and oneness. Jesus has given specific ministries to the church. These ministries are to be for service to all, serving the needs of the whole body of Christ. They are to equip the body of believers to go out and minister in the name of the Lord. This equipping of the saints is meant to edify the body of Christ and to bring us into unity, unity in our faith and our knowledge of Christ. We are one church in Christ and have one Spirit, the Spirit of Jesus and the Father, the Holy Spirit. First Corinthians 12 teaches us:

> For as the body is one and has many members, but all the members of that one body, being many, are one body, so also *is* Christ. For by one Spirit we were all baptized into one body—whether Jews or Greeks, whether slaves or free—and have all been made to drink into one Spirit. For in fact the body is not one member but many.
>
> 1 Corinthians 12:12–14

The Word of God is clear that if we are not rightly aligned with the body of Christ, his church here on earth, we will

Joyce A. Howard

be blown about by every wind of doctrine, always seeking but never receiving. We will be tossed to and fro, always vacillating in our beliefs.

The Lord has given me a church of born-again, Spirit-filled believers who are seeking to walk together into the fullness of Christ. I am glad for the association of this church with the greater apostolic movement taking place in the United States and around the world. I feel connected through this church to the movement of the Lord in our day, the third great awakening and reformation of his church. Just as I must become rightly aligned within a specific body of believers, so must that body be rightly aligned within the whole body of Christ.

"...and take the helmet of salvation..."

Our next piece of armor involves our head. We are to take the helmet of salvation. Salvation (the Greek word *sozo*) means deliverance, safety, liberation, release, preservation, forgiveness, healing, prosperity, rescue, and restoration. God's desire for each one of us is to be delivered, safe, liberated, forgiven, healed, prosperous, and restored. Praise God! Now that is a loving Father!

First Thessalonians 5:7 tells us that our helmet is the hope of salvation. We are saved through faith, but salvation brings hope. The enemy's main point of attack is in our minds, causing us to doubt our salvation and all that it entails. *Faith protects the heart, while hope protects the mind.*

Called to Be Different

189

"…and the sword of the Spirit, which is the word of God…"

So far, all of these pieces of armor have been defensive. Next, we are given an offensive weapon: the sword of the Spirit, which is the word of God. The word here is *rhema*. It is a living word of God communicated to us as a sword in our time of need. The Holy Spirit gives us the *rhema* word of God to speak against an attack. The Spirit brings to our remembrance a particular scripture to use in the time of need. This means we must have God's Word (*logos*) stored in our minds for the Spirit to draw upon.

God's Word pierces and penetrates like a sword. We go on the offensive with God's Word. The book of Hebrews tells us:

> For the word of God *is* living and powerful, and sharper than any two-edged sword, piercing even to the division of soul and spirit, and of joints and marrow, and is a discerner of the thoughts and intents of the heart.
>
> Hebrews 4:12

When Jesus was tempted in the wilderness, he responded by quoting the Word of God. Our response must be like Jesus' response: "It is written." Satan begins by tempting us with "if" statements, trying to create doubt in our minds. He then misquotes or misapplies scriptures, trying to use the Word of God against us. We must know the Word so that we know when he (Satan) is trying to misquote or misapply the Bible.

How does Satan do this? His most common method is through another person who is misquoting or misapplying the scripture. Again, this means we must have God's *logos* Word stored in our minds so that we can recognize what is not truth.

> "…praying always with all prayer and supplication in the Spirit…"

We put on the armor to fight. Prayer is the means by which we fight. Prayer is the means by which we engage in the battle itself and the purpose for which we are armed.

God's Word is our chief weapon employed against Satan. We must study God's Word and prayer. We must know and use God's Word as we pray. *We must pray God's Word back to him.*

Please hear this. We are not unarmed, unable to defend ourselves. We have weapons. We have God's Word and our testimony based upon God's Word. John tells us, "And they overcame him by the blood of the Lamb and by the word of their testimony" (Revelations 12:11a). Praying God's Word back to him is our strongest defense!

> "…being watchful to this end with all perseverance and supplication for all the saints."

Perseverance means we continue in battle until the need is supplied or the provision secured. Sometimes battle requires sleepless vigilance and midnight vigils.

Supplication is our humble appeal to God, who has

the power to grant our request. No soldier would go into battle without learning how to use his weapons. "All prayer" includes intercession, worship, praise, thanksgiving, listening, meditation, praying in tongues, etc.

We must always be battle ready. Warriors run *to* the sound of battle, *not* away from it!

What a mighty call God has given us! What a privilege it is to be able to serve God here on this earth through our everyday lives!

God's Perspective

I shared earlier the experience of when I was baptized in the Holy Spirit, involving Pat Robertson and *The 700 Club*.[61] Right from the moment of my conversion and baptism in the Spirit, a deep hunger for the Word began in me. I could not devour the Bible fast enough nor find enough books, tapes, videos, etc., to learn more. I could not get to prayer meetings and conferences fast enough. I was like a kid who walked into a candy store for the first time and found a big sign saying, "Take all you want! It's free!" I wanted to know everything there was to know about the Lord, his Father, and his Spirit.

A deep and abiding love for the Lord Jesus Christ permeated my being. He felt closer to me than my very breath. I knew I could turn to him for anything and everything. I felt his presence by me when I spent quiet time in prayer and meditation. It was so real and so close that I felt that if I reached out, I would touch him. I felt his comfort and his all-embracing love.

Things were still a mess in my life, but there was no condemnation or holding back on Jesus' part. I knew he loved me totally and completely just as I was and loved me so much that he was going to help me to change my life.

Jesus became the Lord of my life. When I called on his name, my heart cried and my lips spoke the word *Lord*. That is who he was and is to me. He is the Lord of every facet, every nook and cranny of my life. He is the Lord of the good, the bad, and the ugly of my life. He is patiently working with me to right the wrongs and to straighten the pathway on which I walk.

Talking with the Lord became a natural part of my day and life. I knew I could talk with him anytime about anything and that he would be listening. If what I was saying required a response, I knew he would bring it to me. I knew he would speak it into my spirit, show it to me in his Word, or send someone to me with the answer.

Much of the time, speaking in English just did not suffice. I was unable to express the depth of my feelings, concerns, and longings in plain language. And so I often spent time praying in the Spirit to the Lord. This too became a natural part of my day and life.

Prayer stopped being a process of rote memorization or speaking. It became a personal conversation between the God of the universe and me. Wow! Does that blow your mind or what? It sure does mine. To think that the God who created all the heavens and the earth and everything in and on them wanted to hear from me. To think that such a God cared about my little life on planet earth and wanted to be an intimate part of it. Praise to his name! That is so astounding; there are no words I can think of to use that express it.

I have often looked at ant colonies on the ground and thought about God looking down on us human beings. To God, we have to be like what ants look like to us. In fact, the Lord shared a word related to this with me.

See the Ants

Oh my! Oh my! See the ants. See them scurry about. So busy. So self-involved. We are as ants to the Lord. So high above our ways are his ways. So high above our thoughts are his thoughts. The Creator. The one who redeems all. The holy one. And he loves us. Even as we scurry about in our self-importance, he looks over us. He cares about us. He understands how little we grasp of his might. He understands how little we know of his life.

Reach out. Let the father of all fill you. Fill you with his wisdom. Fill you with his knowledge. Fill you with his love. Do not look to one another, but to our God. The mighty Creator. The maker of the heavens and the earth. When God speaks, it is. Whatever he speaks comes into existence. How magnificent! How glorious! Let him share his light and his love with you. Let him share his power with you. The power of his Spirit. The Holy Spirit.

Through him you can do all things. Through him you can rise up and do the things of God as he designed.

The Lord says, "Use the gifts of my Spirit. Flow in them. I release them. I free them in your midst." Freely, the Lord has given the gifts of his Spirit to be our aid, to help us in our need. Speak God's words. They bring life. Speak prophecies, words of wisdom, and words of knowledge. Allow these to come forth out of you. Yes, you! His Spirit dwells in you to make this so. Do not doubt. Do not hesitate. The time for those things is past.

"Behold, I do a new thing!" says the Lord. "I bring it forth now in your midst. Speak out. Obey. See what will happen when you believe and step forth. Step out. I cannot speak through a closed mouth. I cannot speak through lips that do not praise me. I cannot work through a heart that is not centered in me, seeking me above all else.

"Stop your scurrying. Rest in me. Praise me. Put me first. Magnify my name. And then see what I will do in your midst. How I will pour out my blessings upon you. How I will place my hand of protection over you so that no evil can come upon you.

"I AM. Everything exists through me and in me. Every rock and stream and tree, everything responds to me and to my voice. Call out to me. Lift up your prayers as incense to my altar. Pray fervently. Let communion with me be the first order of each new day. Let nothing keep you from seeking me and seeking me first above all else, for I am waiting; I am waiting to pour out my Spirit upon you, upon all who will call on my name, upon all who will seek me first. I am the way and the truth and the life.

"I need you to become obedient—obedient to my Word, obedient to what I have shown you, and obedient to your church leaders. Much is coming, and you must be prepared. Be ready to communicate in strange ways, ways you are not accustomed to using. Plan now. Have systems of communication ready. The time is coming when these will be needed, but they must be made ready now. Do not wait. Do not delay. There will not be time to get ready when the time has come."[62]

The Lord gave me the scene of the ant colony, so at first I was just seeing them. Then the Lord was showing me the gap that exists between us and ants, how far apart we are in design, intelligence, and so much more. The awe of it! The Lord wants us to realize that this is how it is between us and him. He is so much greater than we can ever imagine in our wildest thoughts. How very, very much he loves us despite that gap. He created us so that he could love us. His desire is to bless us. All we have to do is ask and then step out in faith, for he wants to bless us. And he wants to get us prepared. He will not leave his people lost and hurting during these last days. He will stay close and guide us.

So much is happening in our world that never has happened before. We know this to be a part of the Lord's coming. He prepared us in his Word that it would be like this. And he is reminding us now and telling us to get prepared. People have asked me if I felt the Lord was referring to a specific event. I do not. But I know that we need to be ready for these eventualities, situations that would cause us to not be able to meet and situations that would cause us to not be able to communicate by normal methods. If you just think of the effects of Hurricane Katrina, you can see this would be true.[63] Events such as earthquakes, fires, tornados, etc., seem to be very much on the increase in our world. Economic turmoil can lead to civil unrest and riots. We have seen this happen in many countries.

I must stay grounded and steady. I must not allow myself to be distracted by the world around me, nor by my personal circumstances. I must stay in the Word—reading the Word, hearing the Word, and walking in the truths of the Word. I must stay as close to Jesus as I can.

Part of God's call to us is to see the world we live in through his perspective and to see our lives through his eyes. This is not an easy task because our normal view of the world is one of self-centeredness. We view the world with us in the center, like the sun is in the center of our solar system. Let us pray to be able to see as Jesus sees.

Judgment or Revival

I believe God has awakened me, as he is awakening you, so that we can become his mighty end-time army. He wants to bring about revival and restoration throughout this earth. But there are issues to be considered. With revival comes judgment, with judgment comes revival; the two go hand in hand. And the Lord always begins by judging his own people. Here are some of the Lord's concerns, concerns that lead to judgment or revival.

God is concerned about our lukewarm attitudes. Think of the lesson of Joseph—sold into slavery by his brothers who deceived their father. What they intended for evil, God worked for good. Even though Joseph experienced tremendous evil twice, he kept a positive, humble attitude toward God. He believed the Lord would work good out of the failures of his life. Do I hesitate to do what I am called to do because I am afraid of what others will think? Fear of rejection? Do I stay in the comfort of the valley (the testing, trial, or hardship) rather than believe in the power of God through his Spirit to bring me out?

The Lord shared the following with me in May of 2006.

I am shaking! I am shaking! Anything that is not rooted and grounded in me will be exposed. I am doing this corporately throughout the church and individually. I am doing this in you. I have shaken your world and asked the question, "Am I your Lord? Is it I, your Lord, you look to and depend on?" Is your lamp full and ready? Is my lampstand ready?

Only through and with the oil of my Holy Spirit will you be able to hold firm through the quaking power of my coming. I burst forth in fullness through great force, both in the natural and the spiritual. Be prepared. Be ready. For I come. I am the Lord your God and I come. I come for my bride, my church. I come for you.[64]

Along with this word, the Lord gave me this scripture:

> Remember therefore from where you have fallen; repent and do the first works, or else I will come to you quickly and remove your lampstand from its place—unless you repent.
>
> Revelation 2:5

The Lord said that he was shaking corporately throughout the church and individually. I have felt this shaking. I know that he is looking for me to deal with all those areas of my life that I have chosen to ignore, to downplay, or refused to face. He is not trying to punish me; he is trying to heal me and prepare me. He wants to come back for a church that is worthy of his return.

The Lord said that anything that is not rooted and grounded in him will be exposed. This exposure within the world, but more importantly within his church, has been happening at an accelerated pace in the past few years. It is shaking and exposing every pastor and person within the church who is not living in holiness. It is shaking every governmental leader and every economic system within our world. Nothing will be left that the Lord will not shake, for we are meant to comprise a holy church without fault, spot, or wrinkle.

Many of you will feel this shaking (or have already). The shaking will occur until sin and iniquity that have continued in your life are exposed. Are you professing to be a Christian but refusing to forgive others? God will shake you until that is exposed. Are you professing to be a Christian but living like the rest of the world? God will shake and expose that too.

God is concerned about compromise. We are called to be his voice to the world around us. He is concerned about areas where we lower our standards rather than being faithful in our call to holiness. He is concerned about areas where I accept as okay the behaviors and attitudes of other Christians or wrong behaviors and attitudes within myself. Some people who call themselves Christians want to bring the church *down* to their level. They want it to be okay how they spend their time and money. Not forgiving others, refusing to show mercy, and viewing themselves as better than others are okay as long as they go to church on Sunday. Drinking, profanity, and gambling are okay as long as they go to church. The Lord says we are to be holy as he is holy. Without standards of righteousness (right living), we will be no different than Sodom and Gomorrah. (See Genesis 19:1–29.)

In Galatians, the Apostle Paul writes about the works of the flesh.

> Now the works of the flesh are evident, which are: adultery, fornication, uncleanness, lewdness, idolatry, sorcery, hatred, contentions, jealousies, outbursts of wrath, selfish ambitions, dissensions, heresies, envy, murders, drunkenness, revelries, and the like; of which I tell you beforehand, just as I also told *you* in time past, that those who practice such things will not inherit the kingdom of God.
>
> Galatians 5:19–21

Paul wrote this to the Christian churches of Galatia; he was not writing this to unbelievers. He lists works such as idolatry, sorcery, adultery, fornication, murder, and heresy—things that most of us would agree would block a Christian from inheriting the kingdom. However, please notice that he lists other works that many accept as normal such as envy, jealousy, selfish ambition, dissension, drunkenness, and revelry (we would call it "partying"). Paul says these are equally works of the flesh and can block a Christian from inheriting the kingdom.

This is tougher for me to accept. It requires me to search my heart and my soul, and to go humbly before the Lord to seek his mercy and grace. I will never be the light to the world that his Word says I am to be until I open up the hidden crevices of my heart and openly deal with these sins. I cannot be of the world and a Christian at the same time. We are not called to bend to be like the world, but to be a witness to the world of the goodness of the Lord. Are we? I am called to be his voice to my family, friends, neighbors, and fellow workers. Am I?

The Lord often speaks to me by speaking clearly into my spirit and having me write down what he says. His favorite times to do this seem to be in the evening just as I am drifting off to sleep or when I am driving down the road in the car. I am sure he picks these times because they are times when he can have better access to my always-busy mind. I am certain it is because I still do not allow enough quiet time between us for him to be able to speak fully to me. So I have learned to always have a notebook or at least paper and a pencil ready no matter where I am or what I am doing.

I would like to share another word the Lord gave me in June of 2006 concerning judgment.

Judgment is here. Do you not perceive it? It is in the rains and in the wind. It is in the earthquakes and the upheavals. The thunder is its voice. The firmament is its light.

The good will be found. A holy river will flow with their righteous deeds, white and pure and glorious to behold. Evil will come against them, but they will stand strong. They will not bend like the reed in the wind. They will not listen to words that would lead them astray. They will not succumb to hunger or pride.

There will be a mighty army, joined as one. The weak among them will be lifted up. The sick will have hands laid on them and be healed. There will be no poor among them, for those who have will give to those in need. No one will need to beg for anything; help will be given freely. I will speak to my sheep, and they will listen and obey. All will be humble, for all will see it is my hand that guides them and my voice that leads them. Listen. Listen for me. Be ready. For I come.[65]

He gave me this scripture at the same time he gave me this word.

> "And behold, I am coming quickly, and My reward *is* with Me, to give to every one according to his work. I am the Alpha and the Omega, *the* Beginning and *the* End, the First and the Last." Blessed *are* those who do His commandments, that they may have the right to the tree of life, and may enter through the gates into the city. But outside *are* dogs and sorcerers and sexually immoral and murderers and idolaters, and whoever loves and practices a lie. I, Jesus, have sent My angel to testify to you these things in the churches. I am the Root and the Offspring of David, the Bright and Morning Star." And the Spirit and the bride say, "Come!" And let him who hears say, "Come!" And let him who thirsts come. Whoever desires, let him take the water of life freely.
>
> Revelation 22:12–17

God's revival and judgment are contingent upon the people of God getting into order. I see two ways this occurs. First, when we are faithful and obedient, we can count on God to bring salvation to our whole family.

Second, God calls us out of certain places because he needs and wants to judge that place. He cannot judge it until we are gone, as with getting Lot out of Sodom. The compassion of the Lord is upon us. We need to get up, not look behind, and depart to find wherever it is that God is trying to take us to in the Spirit realm. Do not look back to what has been or what could have been. Look forward. Get rid of all excess baggage. If we hesitate, we may miss God's visitation. If necessary, God will send his angels to urge us and push us out of our complacency. Get ready for God's urging angels.

The Lord gave me a further word in July of 2006 concerning judgment.

Weep, my children! Weep! For the harvest has begun. The harvest of all things, the harvest of the wicked, the harvest of the weak, the harvest of the sinful, and the harvest of the just. Yes, it comes. It springs forth. It rains down in thunderings.

Did you hear my words? Did you understand? Every seed sown will come to harvest, to judgment, to justice. Where were you when I spoke? Were you listening? Did you pay attention to my words? Justice will reign down. Judgment will reign down. The fruit will be seen by all. Will it be the fruit of my Spirit? Or will it be the fruit of your flesh, seeds of iniquity? Oh, how I weep. I weep for my church. I weep for my people. Did they not hear? Did they not care? Did they not believe?

The bride must be made ready for my Son, for her bridegroom. Everything that is not of my Spirit, born of my Spirit, must go. I must cleanse the bride. Prepare her. See her just and chaste, purged of her wastefulness and deceit and pride. My justice shall reign. Goodness and mercy shall be the light. Oneness and unity must come, wholeness in me, fullness of my Spirit. Too long you have gone your separate ways, determined in your rightness— so sure, so certain, so wrong.

My body is one. It has many parts. Each part is necessary. Only in wholeness are you one body; fractured and splintered, you are not whole. The eye sees, the ear hears, the leg walks, the arm holds, the hand touches, and the heart brings comfort and love. *Wholeness, be!*

The whole world will be judged, for judgment will come to all. The world did not know that their judgment would come, but you should have known. You should have been prepared. Didn't my word say to watch, to be prepared, to know the hour of your visitation? What seeds did you sow? Have you allowed enmity to exist? Why did you not bring these under salvation, under the cross, under the blood of my Son? Why did you wait? Did my word not tell you "do not delay"? There would not be time at his return?

Weep! Weep, my children! For I weep. I weep for what is undone or half done or never begun. I weep for those who will never know; you were my eyes and my ears and my voice to them. Weep and repent. Seek my forgiveness. For even now I will forgive. Even now I will set free, make whole. Seek me. Seek me with repentant hearts and souls. Confess your sins one to another. Make right. Make whole. Seek unity and wholeness. Seek love. Let go of your prideful ways. Let go of your self-seeking and your self-glory.

Now is the time. For I come in the force of rightness and justice. I come in the voice of judgment. I roar forth in your midst. Hear me. Do not miss this hour of your visitation. See it for what it is. My angels come forth. The trumpet blows. The earth trembles and quakes at my coming. Justice, light the sky! Make a path! Clear the way for the Lord![66]

The Word of God is clear that we must accept the chastening of the Lord, for it is through his chastening that we learn that we are truly the sons and daughters of God. I know what it is like as a mother, grandmother, and college professor to bring about correction to someone. Correction is not always received as it is given—in love. I continually pray for the Lord to keep me open to receiving necessary correction and change in my life so that I may continue to grow up in him.

Jesus is preparing his bride, his church, for his return. He wants us to be pure, without spot or wrinkle or blemish. Jesus is shaking and revealing areas and people within his church that are not in right standing with him. He is allowing sin to be uncovered, sinful areas of Christians' lives that were being kept hidden.

Jesus came to give us life and life more abundantly. He patiently waits for us to be ready. He sees my sin and hardness of heart, and he desires to heal it. He sees yours. Do not wait. Let the Spirit of God heal those hurts and heal your soul now. Jesus is waiting. Healing and wholeness are meant to be yours. The answers are as close to you as your prayer. Reach out right now.

Kingdom Blessings Are Ours

> Do not be deceived, God is not mocked; for whatever a man sows, that he will also reap. For he who sows to his flesh will of the flesh reap corruption, but he who sows to the Spirit will of the Spirit reap everlasting life. And let us not grow weary while doing good, for in due season we shall reap if we do not lose heart. Therefore, as we have opportunity, let us do good to all, especially to those who are of the household of faith.
>
> Galatians 6: 7–10

I had a dream earlier this year. In the dream, I was sleeping. It was a very peaceful sleep, and I awoke feeling very rested. I happened to walk into the kitchen and look out the window. I noticed that the neighbor's house had been flattened. I quickly walked around the house, looking out the various windows. I discovered that all around my house was total destruction. I realized that a tornado had must have come through during the night and wiped everything out, everything but my home. I walked outdoors and looked around. I was in total amazement! Not only was my home okay, but so was my yard, my trees, my flowers, etc. Not a leaf or limb had been touched by the storm. The Lord then spoke to me in the dream and told me that this was because I had blessed and claimed my property as part of his kingdom and that the storms of life could not touch anything that was part of his kingdom.

What a description of what happens when we live our lives dedicated to the Lord and are led by his Spirit versus fleshly, selfish lives. How blessed we are when we freely choose to allow the Holy Spirit to control of our lives.

The blessings of the Lord are righteousness, peace, and joy in the Holy Spirit (Romans 14:17). He watches over us to bless us. When we walk in his Spirit, listening for and to his voice, he guides us. Goodness and mercy are ours. The more we submit to his will in our lives, the more fruitful our lives become. Praise God!

The Call Nashville

The Lord has dealt with me on my perspective of the world in which we live. He has led me to look beyond the current state of our world, to gain a historical perspective of it. What I found was shocking, to put it mildly. Two of the main tools he used to bring me to this awareness were *The Call Nashville* and a movie called *Time Changer*.

The Call Nashville occurred on 7/7/07 in Nashville, Tennessee, in Titans Stadium.[67] It was organized under the leadership of Lou Engle.[68] It was a day of fasting, prayer, repentance, and worship. The focus of the day was to gather before the Lord to repent and cry out to the Lord to forgive the sins of America and to forgive the sins of each of us gathered there. We denounced involvement with the sins of Baal that abound in our world. Baal worship involved sacrificing sons and daughters to Baal. In

Called to Be Different

our day, we sacrifice our children to abortion, rebellion, pornography, other sexual lusts and perversions, greed, addictions, compulsions, etc. During that day, we cried out to the Lord to forgive us and our nation. Once we had repented, we then remarried the Lord (recovenanted with the Lord) in our hearts and lives.

In the evening, using shofars, drums, the rattling of keys, and our voices, we released the sound to heaven of the third great awakening in America. It was a life-changing day! For me personally, it was another of those days that Patricia Beall Gruits had taught us about, a deepening experience with key touches along the way, moments of further conversion.[69]

In preparation for the day, we were called to a Daniel fast for forty days. My sister and I, along with other friends, agreed in prayer to do the fast. We received a prayer focus for the fast through Chuck Pierce's ministry.[70]

We are told about Daniel's eating habits in the book of Daniel chapter one. Daniel asked that he and his friends be allowed to eat just vegetables and water, abstaining from the delicacies and wines served in Babylon.

As we met during those forty days, we were amazed at how the Lord honored us to maintain the fast. For each of us, it was a time of drawing closer to the Lord in prayer and through his Word. We were revitalized. We were able to obtain Dutch Sheets's teaching series on Baal, which blessed and taught us and opened our eyes even further to see the condition of our world.[71]

Since that day, I have heard Chuck Pierce share that 7/7/07 was the day that the tip of the sword of the Lord touched earth.[72] He said that nothing would ever be the same again. I know that is definitely true for my life. And I believe it is true for America.

I believe we are in the first days of the third great awakening. This awakening will continue to shake our worlds, individually and corporately. It will shake our families, churches, and cities. It will shake our nation and then, from there, the nations of the world.

Perhaps what stayed with me the most from 7/7/07 are the testimonies of a couple who were involved in the sexual revolution of 1967. The wife shared how they actually believed they were releasing love and freedom to our world only to discover over time that they had been deceived. She shared her loss of innocence, first use of drugs, etc. She shared about the generation gap that grew between herself and her parents. She then shared the horror and sorrow she has felt over the past forty years as she witnessed the explosion of sin and the loss of moral values that were fueled by their summer of love.

We have been like the Israelites who rebelled against the Lord, wandering in the desert of our sin, rebellion, and perversion for the past forty years. Those of us gathered at *The Call*, estimated to be over seventy thousand people, repented together for this turning away from God that occurred forty years ago. Like the Israelites, we confessed our sin and asked the Lord's forgiveness. We prayed that we, as individuals and a nation, would no longer have to wander in the desert of our sin.

Called to Be Different

Time Changer

I returned from Nashville in a deep time of reflection on the tremendous changes that have occurred in our world over the past forty years. The Lord led me to the movie *Time Changer*.[73] If you have not seen this movie or have not seen it since its first release, I recommend that you view it as a means of reflection upon the changes in our world. It is set in the late 1890s, a little over one hundred years ago, in America. It accurately reflects the culture of that day—the dress, lifestyle, moral values, attitudes, etc., of that society.

One of the characters is thrust forward to our day (early 2000s). He is appalled, repulsed, and shocked by what he sees and hears. He cannot believe what is accepted as the norm in our society.

He is most appalled by the attitude and actions of our churches. He comes to the conclusion that the true gospel message must be preached again within the supposed churched. He realizes that most of the people who are showing up each week for services have no idea who Jesus is; they have no personal knowledge or relationship with the Lord. They have never repented and asked Jesus into their hearts, bringing their sin and lives to the cross of Calvary and under Jesus' blood. In fact, many have no desire to do so. They believe that simple attendance at church once a week will save them. Their moral compass is whatever feels right for them; if it feels good, do it.

When you watch this man agonize over the world he sees, you realize how far off course we have become as God's people. This is perhaps one of Satan's greatest deceptions. He has lulled us to the point that we think belonging to a church is enough. Members in every denominational and nondenominational church are falling under this deception. Many people truly believe that as long as they have been baptized by a church, sporadically attend, and give money to that church that they are assured of heaven. It is referred to as "fire insurance," as they are safe from the fires of hell.

How do I know this is happening? I have been to church gatherings where there is nothing to do with the life and love of the Lord present. Instead, there is gambling, beer tents, non-Christian rock bands, etc., all in the name of raising money for the church. This is a common practice in our day. Our supposed church gatherings, gatherings in which we represent the Lord, are no different than gatherings that occur in the world at large—the world of nonbelievers.

In many cases, our dress is no different. Women, especially, dress in the low-cut, seductive clothing that the world has generated. They have no qualms about dressing this way for church gatherings.

Our language is often just as colorful as that of the world's. I have been around many churchgoers who freely swear and feel it is a sign of their manhood (even though some are female), even going to the point of freely using the Lord's name in vain. They do not realize what an offense it is to the Lord, that it is a violation of his third commandment. I have been there myself. I have gone through a period in my life where I was caught up in this same deception.

I have been in church situations or among Christians

where the prevailing attitude is like that of the Pharisees toward Jesus. The Pharisees had come to believe so totally in their many laws that they no longer offered forgiveness and mercy. They were angry when Jesus healed on the Sabbath (for breaking their tradition) rather than rejoicing that a fellow human had been set free.

The character in the movie concludes that sinners abound within the Lord's body, his church here on earth. Yes, we are all sinners saved by grace. But that does not mean we are to openly continue in a lifestyle of sin once we have given our hearts to the Lord. More often, it is a sign that we really have not done that—given our hearts to him. It is a sign that we are going through the motions but without the revelation of the heart.

Preparing His Bride

We must get the bride ready. We must get Jesus' church, his body here on earth, his bride, ready to meet him. We must recognize the signs where our churches have become a reproach to the Lord and repent. We can no longer call people to join our churches as if they were joining a country club to simply live their lives in the same manner they were before.

People come to the church—and often to us as individual Christians—hungry, searching. They come because they recognize a need in their hearts and lives. Their need is not to gather to learn how to scrapbook or to play on a church sports league or to gamble, drink, and party. They can fulfill those needs out in the world. Not that it is wrong to have things such as church sports leagues or women's groups, as long as they are secondary to the call to a personal relationship with the Lord and are not the focus of the church's activity.

The hunger that draws people is a hunger for a relationship with God, a relationship with our Savior, Jesus Christ. They are hungry for the peace and joy that only comes through communion with a triune God that takes up residence in our hearts and wants to be in daily relationship with us. They are hungry for the reality of Jesus and his Spirit. They come desiring to experience the fullness of who God is and wants to be in their personal lives.

Church attendance should not be drudgery. It should not be the most boring hour people spend in their week. Church attendance should represent a time when we corporately gather to celebrate what we experience with the Lord the other one hundred sixty-seven hours of the week. In fact, if we are busy timing our gathering to just one hour, that is a sign the celebration of the Spirit of the Lord's presence is not what is drawing us to gather.

Too long we have settled for ritual rather than relationship. Too long we have allowed tradition to dominate our actions. We have lulled ourselves to the point where our services are either unrecognizable as an instrument of the Lord or so filled with religious tradition that they are a turnoff to the average seeker.

These revelations have caused me to reflect anew on my own life. If a seeker looks at me, does he or she see anything different? Or do I look just like the world? If a seeker listens to me, does he or she hear words that magnify the Lord? Or do I sound just like the world? They are

Called to Be Different

215

seeking the Lord. Is there anything in my walk, my talk, or the way I live my life that witnesses to the presence of the Lord in my life?

Do I truly know the Lord? Do I sit in his presence? Do I feel his comfort and his love? Does he speak to me through his Spirit and through his Word? Do I have a hunger for his Word? What does my life look like to an outsider, a seeker, a pre-believer? Is there anything about me that attracts them not to me, but to the Lord?

I heard Pastor Barbara Yoder say the following, "If there is true intimacy with Christ, there will be transformation."[74] In other words, conversion leads to transformation; justification leads to sanctification.

Conversely, if there is no transformation, it is a sign that there is no intimacy. It is a sign that true conversion has not occurred. Many people join the church; they do not marry the Lord. They do not give their hearts and lives to the Lord, covenanting with the Lord. They simply agree to join a church community, as if it were the better choice of a country club.

Where are you on this scale? Where am I? Has Jesus become the Lord of your life? Of my life? Have our values, goals, actions, and desires changed? Or have we simply fit them into the paradigm of the current church community? Not what the church was like one hundred years ago or even forty years ago, but the paradigm of many of the churches of our day?

Repentance Must Begin Within the Lord's Church

Please let me share the following descriptions with you. The first is Jesus' commissioning to the disciples. It is what he told them to do and be as the church, as his body, his bride. The Gospel of Mark records:

> And He said to them, "Go into all the world and preach the gospel to every creature. He who believes and is baptized will be saved; but he who does not believe will be condemned. And these signs will follow those who believe: In My name they will cast out demons; they will speak with new tongues; they will take up serpents; and if they drink anything deadly, it will by no means hurt them; they will lay hands on the sick, and they will recover."
>
> Mark 16:15–18

This next description is also Jesus speaking to his disciples. It is his description of what many of his supposed followers in his bride, his church, will look like at the time of his second coming. The Gospel of Matthew records Jesus' words:

> But as the days of Noah *were,* so also will the coming of the Son of Man be. For as in the days before the flood, they were eating and drinking, marrying and giving in marriage, until the day that Noah entered the ark, and did not know until the flood came and took them all away, so also will the coming of the Son of Man be.
>
> Matthew 24:37–39

Jesus is describing what the very reality of the church is today. He continues to exhort them with the following:

> Then two *men* will be in the field: one will be taken and the other left. Two *women will be* grinding at the mill: one will be taken and the other left. Watch therefore, for you do not know what hour your Lord is coming. But know this, that if the master of the house had known what hour the thief would come, he would have watched and not allowed his house to be broken into. Therefore you also be ready, for the Son of Man is coming at an hour you do not expect.
>
> Matthew 24:40–44

I say to you, the Lord's house has been broken into! The bride is not ready for the bridegroom! Repentance must begin within the house of the Lord. Jesus is not coming back for the world; he is coming back for his church, the body of Christ. His desire is that we wake up as a body of believers and purify our own hearts, lives, and households. His desire is that we purify his church.

Jesus calls us to hear again the words of his Great Commission to go out in his power and his love to save the lost within our world. To do this, we must first save the lost within our churches so that we again see the things that Jesus described in Mark 16.

> "And these signs will follow those who believe: In My name they will cast out demons; they will speak with new tongues; they will take up ser-

pents; and if they drink anything deadly, it will by no means hurt them; they will lay hands on the sick, and they will recover."

Mark 16:17–18

A Call to God's Word

We must return to the Word of God. We must accept and believe in the entirety of the Scriptures. Jesus does not tell us that we can pick and choose from among these sacred writings, choosing those that fit our desires and casting aside others. Nothing gives us that right. We must believe in all that has been written, as it is God's Word to us to guide our lives. We must accept the account of creation just as we accept the account of Jesus' death and resurrection.

We cannot water down or compromise God's Word. We cannot say that we will believe in the account of creation but change it to fit the current world's belief in evolution. The ideas behind evolution came through the writings of a man, Charles Darwin.[75] They were not inspired by God; they were simply the ideas of a man.

This idea of compromise, blending creation and evolution into one belief, has worked its way past the classrooms and texts of our public schools and colleges. This idea of compromise is now found in many of the teachings within our churches. I was taught this blended belief back in the eighties while studying at the Catholic regional seminary. This compromised teaching appeared in the religious education materials and texts used by students in the religious education programs I oversaw.

In fact, this idea has become so common and ingrained

into our minds through public and Christian education that the majority of us do not even realize it has happened. We do not even realize that our beliefs have been deceptively compromised.

So I ask you, what do you believe with regard to creation? Do you believe there is one true God in heaven, one triune God existing as our Father, Jesus, and the Holy Spirit, and that he and he only is the Creator of this universe and all that is within it? And do you believe it was created as the Scriptures tell us it was created within six days? And that man was created by God on that sixth day? And that man was created in the image and likeness of God, as recorded in Genesis? Or do you believe as the evolutionists believe that man evolved from apes? And that life evolved out of the primordial mud of the earth through a lightning strike or through seeded crystals?

A Call to God's Standards

As you now know, I was pregnant when I began my first marriage. I would like to tell you about the evening of the day I found out that I was pregnant. I was very much in shock. I was afraid and angry with God and the world in general. I did not know what to do. Because of things I have written about here, calling my parents for their help did not seem like a viable option.

I want to give credit to my first husband. When I broke the news to him, he immediately said that we would marry. That sounds like the perfect answer, right? However, up to that point, our relationship had been about having fun with our friends, drinking, partying, etc. This was not a courting situation where marriage was seriously being considered.

That evening I went off by myself and began walking. This was a college town; it was not a place where a young single woman should have been walking alone after dark. Nevertheless, I went. I walked around for hours. I found an open area where I could scream and vent some of my anger at the Lord, as if it was his fault I had made the decisions I had.

One thing was certain through it all: abortion was not an option. Of course, it is true that at that point in the history of our country, abortions were not as easy to get. But ease was not my concern. I knew right from the start that a new little life was forming in my body. This was going to be my child, my daughter or son; I had no idea which.

I have always loved biology. I studied biology in both high school and college. I had looked at enough drawings, read enough information, and saw enough videos that I knew that life began right from the moment of conception. I was aware how soon into the process the characteristics of that tiny baby could begin to be seen.

More than that, I knew that God was the author of all life. I knew that this tiny baby could not and would not be forming in my womb if God's hand had not been involved in the process. I knew that if I did anything to stop that process, it would be murder. And not just random murder—it would be the murder of my own child.

The lies of abortion rule in our day. Every day babies are ripped and torn from the wombs of their mothers. Even babies that survive the horror of an abortion are often left without needed medical care, discarded as if they are rag dolls. We in our country will have to answer to God for legalizing the killing of innocent babies, either when we stand before his throne or through judgments he will release upon our nation.

Thankfully, the Lord has an angelic service that immediately sweeps these innocent babies up and carries them to his throne. They are loved and cherished in heaven.

Often, abortion is not the choice of the girl or woman who is carrying the baby. The fathers sometimes demand it, and even parents demand it. I know many women who did not know any different or were simply too afraid to face what was going to come. I do not condemn these women. I have compassion for them. I have stood in their shoes, and I know that I have absolutely no right to judge.

As Christians, we have stood idly by and allowed this to happen in our world. We have let the lies escalate to the point they sound realistic and truthful. Lies such as, "It isn't really a baby until it is born," "The woman has a right to do what she wants with her own body," and "This prevents an unwanted baby from having to live a life where its care is uncertain."

Do you know anyone who was adopted? Ted's father was. Had his birth mother decided to abort Ted's father (rather than put him up for adoption), Ted and all his family would never have been born. When I think of the beautiful people that make up his family—his brothers, sisters, nieces, and nephews—I shudder to think that they might never have been given life.

A whole generation of people have had their lives snuffed out before they even drew their first breath in this world. Not only were their lives snuffed out, but so too were the children, grandchildren, and future generations that would have flowed out of their lives. Artists, teachers, preachers, scientists, researchers, prophets, and evangelists—snuffed out.

But God's Word has not changed. And God's standards have not changed. Unless we stand as the people of God and work to right this evil within our society, our generation will be judged for it. We must accept our complacency with this sin. We must repent and then fight to change the laws within our land that allow abortion.

If you have read any of the Old Testament, you are aware that a people can be judged when they knowingly allow grievous sin to occur in their presence. We are called to right this sin in our world. We are called to reinstate God's standards concerning life here in America and around the world.

There is the issue in our day of the definition of marriage. God's Word is clear where he stands on the subjects of homosexuality and homosexual marriage. God instituted marriage to be between a man and a woman. He gave heterosexual couples the unique ability, opportunity, and blessing to bring children into the world. Marriage is meant to be a sacred covenant between one man, one woman, and God.

Genesis 18 and 19 tell the story of Sodom and Gomorrah.

> But before they retired for the night, all the men of Sodom, young and old, came from all over the city and surrounded the house. They shouted to Lot,

> "Where are the men who came to spend the night with you? Bring them out to us so we can have sex with them!"
>
> Genesis 19:4–5 (NLT)

God responded to the sexual sin of these cities. We are told:

> Then the Lord rained down fire and burning sulfur from the sky on Sodom and Gomorrah. He utterly destroyed them, along with the other cities and villages of the plain, wiping out all the people and every bit of vegetation.
>
> Genesis 19:24–25 (NLT)

This is recorded in Leviticus: "Do not practice homosexuality, having sex with another man as with a woman. It is a detestable sin" (Leviticus 18:22, NLT).

The issues of homosexual relations and sexual sin come up in the New Testament in 1 Corinthians 6:9–10, 2 Peter 2:4–10, Romans 1:8–32, and Jude 1:6–7. I encourage you to check them out.

God views all sexual activities that are outside of his ordained Word as sin, not just homosexuality. But Sodom and Gomorrah were the only cities recorded as being totally wiped out by God because of their sexual sin (with the exception of Lot and his family, whom God spared for the sake of Abraham).

My place as a Christian is to love everyone. I do not get to judge people according to their sin. If I were to do that, I would come under the same judgment that I was using. "Judge not, that you be not judged" (Matthew 7:1). People involved in homosexuality are God's children, sons and daughters, that Jesus died on the cross for. Jesus loves them just as much as he loves you and me.

I happen to have friends, who have been my friends for years, who are involved in homosexual relationships. I do not love them any less than I do other friends. These friends know where I stand on God's Word, but I do not let that come between how I relate to them—with dignity. God says I can hate the sin, but I must love the sinner.

I must constantly speak God's Word as life to the sinner. This is what people did for me. My sins, although perhaps not as blatant and obvious (or maybe they were), were just as detestable to God. And yet others loved me. Jesus loved me. Jesus loved me enough to wait with me until I was ready and able to hear, repent, and accept his forgiveness.

So we must work as a people to right the laws that exist allowing for abortion and homosexual marriage. We must correct these evils or face the judgment that is coming. At the same time, we must love the sons and daughter of God who are involved in these sins, the same way that we want the Lord and others to love us.

A Call to Reawaken

I would like to share Jesus' last words to us from the book of Revelation. In Revelation 22, Jesus says:

> "And behold, I am coming quickly, and My reward *is* with Me, to give to every one according

to his work. I am the Alpha and the Omega, *the* Beginning and *the* End, the First and the Last."

"I, Jesus, have sent My angel to testify to you these things in the churches. I am the Root and the Offspring of David, the Bright and Morning Star."

Revelation 22:12–13, 16

Finally, Jesus says, "He who testifies to these things says, 'Surely I am coming quickly'" (Revelation 22:20a). To this, John responds, "Amen. Even so, come, Lord Jesus!" (Revelation 22:20b).

We must hear this call of the Lord to reawaken and prepare ourselves and his church, his body, his bride, for his return.

Called to Be Different

Since February 26, 1976, I have been preparing to meet the Lord. On that day, when I accepted Jesus as my personal Savior, he became the Lord of my life. Through his blood, I became acceptable to God, my father and the creator of the universe. To God, I became holy, blameless, and above reproach. Not because of anything I did or could do in the future, but because of what Jesus did for me in his death on the cross. His blood is what makes me acceptable, only his blood.

When I accepted Jesus as my Savior, I confessed my sins to him. I confessed that I was filled with sin, the product of a sinful world. Jesus accepted my confession and my cry. He put my sins under his blood so that when God the Father looks at me, all he sees is the blood of his son. When he looks at me, I am not just free from blemish (faultless) but also free from the charge of it—above reproach.

This status with God the Father comes with a condition. The condition is that I stay rooted and grounded in the faith and hope of the Gospel. Jesus tells us, "'I am the vine, you *are* the branches. He who abides in Me, and I in him, bears much fruit; for without Me you can do nothing" (John 15:5). I must remain settled, steadfast in my relationship with the Lord. I must not shift or move away from him. This implies an inner strength that I must possess.

I love how Colossians 1:21–23 reads in *The Message Bible*:

> You yourselves are a case study of what he does. At one time you all had your backs turned to God, thinking rebellious thoughts of him, giving him trouble every chance you got. But now, by giving himself completely at the Cross, actually dying for you, Christ brought you over to God's side and put your lives together, whole and holy in his presence. You don't walk away from a gift like that! You stay grounded and steady in that bond of trust, constantly tuned in to the Message, careful not to be distracted or diverted. There is no other Message—just this one. Every creature under heaven gets this same Message. I, Paul, am a messenger of this Message.
>
> Colossians 1: 21–23 (MSG)

Our Stance

I am beginning to see the Lord's hand more clearly in the events that have happened in my life. What a joy! I want

Joyce A. Howard

to share with you a scripture, 2 Corinthians 6:3–10, which I believe the Lord has given to me and is meant for us. I'm going to illustrate it as a teaching using the New Living Translation and going through its points.

First, we live in such a way that no one will stumble because of us or find fault because of our ministry. We patiently endure troubles and hardships and calamities of every kind. We have been beaten, beaten down by circumstances. We have been put in prison, prisons of our own making, such as pride or jealousy or lust. We have faced angry mobs: parents, spouses, children, grandchildren, or co-workers. We have worked to exhaustion caring for our families and meeting our many commitments. We have endured sleepless nights, sleepless watching. We have gone without food, fasting and praying for the Lord.

It is our purity, understanding, knowledge, spiritual insight, patience, kindness, and sincere love that witnesses to the Holy Spirit within us. We faithfully speak the truth, allowing God's power to work in us. We use the weapon of righteousness in the right hand for attack as a sword and in the left hand for defense as a shield. We serve God whether people honor us or despise us, whether they slander us or praise us.

This is our stance. We are honest whether we are called impostors and branded as deceivers or are vindicated as truthful and honest. We are ignored, unknown by the world, even though we are well known to God. We live close to death, but we are still alive; as dying, and yet here we are alive. We have been beaten and chastened by suffering, but we have not been killed. Our hearts ache, but we always have joy—

Called to Be Different

grieved and mourning, yet always rejoicing. We are poor, but we give spiritual riches to others. We own nothing, and yet we have everything, as if possessing all.

> Our work as God's servants gets validated—or not—in the details. People are watching us as we stay at our post, alertly, unswervingly...in hard times, tough times, bad times; when we're beaten up, jailed, and mobbed; working hard, working late, working without eating; with pure heart, clear head, steady hand; in gentleness, holiness, and honest love; when we're telling the truth, and when God's showing his power; when we're doing our best setting things right; when we're praised, and when we're blamed; slandered, and honored; true to our word, though distrusted; ignored by the world, but recognized by God; terrifically alive, though rumored to be dead; beaten within an inch of our lives, but refusing to die; immersed in tears, yet always filled with deep joy; living on handouts, yet enriching many; having nothing, having it all.
>
> 2 Corinthians 6:3–10 (MSG)

Praise God! What a call! We are so blessed of the Lord! Stand tall! Stand firm! Let nothing sway you from your call!

The Seasons of Our Lives

God our Father is a God of seasons in our lives. Ecclesiastes describes this for us. After all, where did time in all its dimensions come from if not from God, the Creator of all? Recognizing this fact means that we need to view all

Joyce A. Howard

aspects of time—the hours of the day, weeks, months, years, seasons on the earth, and the seasons in our lives—from God's perspective.

> To everything *there is* a season, A time for every purpose under heaven: A time to be born, And a time to die; A time to plant, And a time to pluck *what is* planted; A time to kill, And a time to heal; A time to break down, And a time to build up; A time to weep, And a time to laugh; A time to mourn, And a time to dance; A time to cast away stones, And a time to gather stones; A time to embrace, And a time to refrain from embracing; A time to gain, And a time to lose; A time to keep, And a time to throw away; A time to tear, And a time to sew; A time to keep silence, And a time to speak; A time to love, And a time to hate; A time of war, And a time of peace.
>
> Ecclesiastes 3:1–8

How we are created is not an accident. The fact that a tiny egg and sperm can come together to create a new life is by design. We each began as this tiny life source. Everything that we needed to grow and become who we are today was there at that point of union between our mother and father. That does not mean everything about our creation was perfect, but we were not an accident. When life occurs, our Creator God is intimately involved. God personally breathes life into every baby at the point of conception.

Scripture tells us that even before we were formed in our mother's womb, God knew us. Isn't that something!

Called to Be Different

In fact, Scripture tells us that we were in God's heart and God's plan even before the world came into existence. That is powerful. If you have ever struggled with low self-worth, meditate on that fact. God had decided on and planned your existence before he created the world.

So everything in God's creation involves times and seasons and cycles. At birth, we are dependent on others. As we grow, we learn to stand on our own. We each pass through times where independence and dependence compete in our lives. "Me! Me! Me!" becomes a dominant mantra. It is a period (time, season) that we must pass through until we come to understand the intrinsic value of others. Until we learn to choose to be dependable, a person that family, friends, and others can look to for support and help and love. Instead of us constantly needing, we become the person that others can depend upon.

Sometimes this is expressed within our families, with our children and grandchildren or with aging parents. We cycle through these various seasons of dependence. And as we cycle, we discover the mystery of God's plan. We discover how our Father designed us to love and be loved.

These cycles exist within God's family. At the appointed time, God chose Abraham. From him, God formed the Jewish people: Israel. In the fullness of time, God brought his Son into the world. Jesus was the Christ, the Anointed One, the long-awaited Messiah. However, Jesus did not come in the way the Jewish people were expecting him to come: as an earthly ruler. Therefore, the bulk of the Jewish people of his day did not recognize or accept him.

The early believers were led by the Holy Spirit to reach

out to the other people of that day, the Gentiles, as well as the Jews. Over time, we became known as Christians, the followers of Christ. It was as if God's original family, the Jews, birthed a stepfamily, the Christians. And both these families, followers of the one true God, continue to this day.

You may want to ask, how could this happen? How could God's family be divided? This may be a real question and concern for you. All I have to do is look at my family and I understand. I have stepgrandchildren. My own children were stepchildren. There are stepchildren and stepgrandchildren throughout my parents' generation, my generation, etc.

Over time, God's Jewish family was dispersed around the world. The land that was given to Abraham to become Israel passed through varied ownership. Around the start of the last century (early 1900s), God began to call the Jewish people back to Israel.[76] He worked through men and circumstances to cause this to come about. In 1948 Israel became a nation again.[77] In 1967 the Jewish people were able to reclaim most of Jerusalem as theirs.[78]

So what was God doing during this same timespan with his stepfamily, his adopted family? In the early 1900s, the Holy Spirit was poured out with signs, wonders, and miracles to a tiny group of believers gathered at Azusa Street in Los Angeles, California.[79] From this small beginning, revival began to spread across the world.

Around the year 1948, a new level of evangelism and healing ministry came forth. Oral Roberts, Billy Graham, William Branham, and others began filling tents and then stadiums with revival meetings and healing crusades.[80]

Many of our great Christian leaders of today can trace their roots to that period of time.

Then in 1967 the charismatic renewal broke out.[81] It spread from the Catholic Church through every other denominational church that existed. The reality of the gifts and power of the Holy Spirit were experienced again as they were on the day of Pentecost when the church was first birthed.

And so time marches on. God's people march on. Today, more so than at any other time in our history, the people of God are becoming aware of their roots. Many Jewish people have come to accept Jesus as their Messiah. Many Christian people have come to accept the Jewish people as part of God's family. Clearly, we seem to be entering a new level in our understanding and relationship with God and one another.

In 2007 two major fortieth anniversary celebrations occurred: Jerusalem's return to the people of Israel, and the Holy Spirit's awakening of the Christian church. Prophets, apostles, evangelists, pastors, and teachers have become evident again throughout the church, operating again as we see them in the book of Acts.

God our Father is speaking again through his prophets. He is telling us that this is the time he will hear our prayers and heal our families. This is the time to draw near to the Lord and ask him for the salvation of members of your family, for those who have lost themselves in the midst of independence, and for those who have been unable to reconnect with God and family, that they will accept the blessings of dependence and love.

God has not changed us as human beings. God does

not change. We are still created in the image of God. Scripture says, "Male and female he created us." And he gave us dominion over the rest of his creation. That dominion must flow from our revelation of our understanding and love for our Creator.

May the Lord Jesus Christ be manifested in your life. May you experience all the blessings of being his child: love, healing, deliverance, and oneness. May his glory shine through your life during this time as never before.

Jesus' Call to Us

I would like to end with the same thought I began this book with. *You and I are called to be different.* Different in how we live our everyday lives and relate to the people around us, by the choices we make in how we will use our time and money, by the things we will expose our eyes and ears and minds to, by how we grieve the loss of a loved one, by how we view our retirement years, and by all the actions of our lives. *We are called out of the world, not to behave as the rest of the world does.*

I exhort you to seek the Lord; accept his call to be his disciple. Ask him to be your Savior and the Lord of your everyday life. Ask him to baptize you in his Holy Spirit so that you can walk with the favor, blessings, power, and fruit of his Spirit every day of your life. Ask him to guide you into becoming a light in your world to family and friends and in your neighborhood, church, and community. Accept his call to bring seekers and prebelievers into the glorious kingdom of his light. We need to be assured of heaven, where we will dwell for all of eternity, but we also need to be a light for him right here, right now on this earth. *May his kingdom come and his will be done on earth as it is in heaven.*

Salvation Prayer

I have shared with you how I grew up in the church. As a young child, I was baptized. I attended church, Sunday school, and our church's youth group. But the fact of the matter is that I did not have a personal relationship with Jesus. For whatever reason, I had been unable to truly hear the Gospel message. I was always hungry and seeking—just trying to find the answer somewhere else. It is very possible that you have been in this same situation. Circumstances in your life may have kept you from being able to hear the message and respond. There are many versions of what we call "the sinner's prayer." I chose the following one to share because it was Ted's favorite. He was fully aware that we are living in the last days and prayed that each of you would be ready for the second coming of Jesus Christ. Or if your death were to come first (as it did for him), he wanted to be certain you would be ready to meet Jesus.

If you have never prayed and asked the Lord Jesus to come into your heart and take over your life, you can do that right now. Please pray this prayer to our Lord. He is waiting for you with open arms. He desires for you to be freed from your burden of sin. He desires to pour out his love within you. Here it is:

Lord Jesus, I need you. I am tired of living for myself and going my own way. Thank you for dying on the cross for my sins. I repent of my sins and open my heart to you. I receive you right now as my Savior and Lord. Thank you for forgiving me and giving me eternal life. Fill me with your Holy Spirit and make me the kind of person you want me to be. Let the gifts and fruit of your Holy Spirit flow through me so that others will come to know you. Amen.

Holy Spirit Baptism

It is possible that you received Jesus into your heart earlier in your life (were "born again") but have discovered that you are not living your life the way that our Lord desires. It may be that you have not understood the call on our lives to spread the Gospel and bring others into God's kingdom. Or you may recognize that you lack the power to do so. If you have come to know Jesus as your Savior but have never prayed for God to fill you with his Holy Spirit, you can do that now too.

Lord Jesus, I ask you to release the power of your Spirit in me. Holy Spirit, I ask you to make yourself known to me. Holy Spirit, help me to know you as well as I know Jesus and my Father. Holy Spirit, please release your gifts and fruit into my life. I ask you to bless me with your heavenly prayer language so that I too can speak the mysteries of God back to my Father. Holy Spirit, may you become the dominating force in my life. Amen.

Called to Be Different

Addendum

Things God Won't Ask on That Day
(Author Unknown)

God won't ask what kind of car you drove; He'll ask how many people you drove who didn't have transportation.

God won't ask the square footage of your house; He'll ask how many people you welcomed into your house.

God won't ask about the clothes you had in your closet; He'll ask how many people you helped to clothe.

God won't ask the color of your skin; He'll ask about the content of your character.

God won't ask what your job title was; He'll ask if you performed your job to the best of your ability.

God won't ask how many friends you had; He'll ask how many people to whom you were a friend.

God won't ask in what neighborhood you lived; He'll ask how you treated your neighbors.

God won't ask what your highest salary was; He'll ask if you compromised your character to obtain it.

Joyce A. Howard

Endnotes

1. Karen S. Williams, Author of *Elegy For A Scarred Shoulder*, Willow Books, 2008; Cave Canem African-American Poetry Fellow; 2009 *Poets and Writers Magazine* Debut Poet; http://www.kswpoetry.com/index.html

2. Pat Robertson and The 700 Club, viewed on February 26, 1976, http://www.cbn.com/

3. Jack Hayford's VHS series, *You and Your Angels*; notes dated January 22, 2006, http://www.jackhayford.org/

4. Master of Theological Studies, granted May, 1984, St. John's Provincial Seminary, formerly located in Plymouth, MI, http://www.archdioceseofdetroit.org/StJohn/About+Us+15400/History.htm

5. "The Life of Theodore August Paul Howard," July 18, 2004, by Joyce Howard and Riky Drenovsky

6. Kenneth Copeland, *The Wake-Up Call* DVD, August 26, 2004, KCM Ministries, http://www.kcm.org/

7. Billy Joe and Sharon Daugherty, *Victory in Jesus* television program, July 15, 2005, http://www.victory.com/VIJ/

8. Billy Joe and Sharon Daugherty, Victory Christian Center website, http://www.victory.com/

9. Billy Joe and Sharon Daugherty, Victory Bible Institute (VBI), http://www.vbitulsa.org/

10. *The Best of the GVB (Gaither Vocal Band)* CD, 2004, Gaither Music Group, http://www.gaither.com/

11. "A Brand New Song" by Woody Wright, Song #8, Disc One, *The Best of the GVB (Gaither Vocal Band)* CD, 2004, Gaither Music Group

12. Water baptism, April 12, 2006, Lamb of God Fellowship, Montrose, MI, http://www.logf.org/pwsite/

13. *Landmines in the Pathway of the Believer* VHS series, Dr. Charles Stanley, In Touch Ministries, notes dated January 1, 2006, http://www.intouch.org/site/c. dhKHIXPKIuE/b.2264355/

14. Kenneth Copeland, April 25, 2006, Azusa Street Centennial, Crenshaw Christian Center, LA, CA, http://www.streamingfaith.com/directory/network. aspx?nsn=AZUSAODC

15. Kenneth Copeland, *The Wake-Up Call* DVD, August 26, 2004, KCM Ministries, http://www.kcm.org/

Joyce A. Howard

16. *Intimacy* definition, Microsoft Encarta College Dictionary, 2001, St. Martin's Press, New York

17. *Footprints in the Sand*, poem by Mary Stevenson, 1936, footprints-inthe-sand.com website

18. *Protecting Your Home From Spiritual Darkness* Book, Chuck D. Pierce and Rebecca W. Sytsema, 2004, Regal Books, Ventura, CA, http://www.glory-of-zion.org/index.htm

19. *One Night With the King* Movie, Fox Faith, 2006, http://www.foxfaith.com/

20. *Hadassah-One Night With the King* Novel, Tommy Tenney, 2004, http://www.tommytenney.com/

21. Dennis Cummings, Warrior Heart Ministries, South Lyon, Michigan, warrior.heart1@yahoo.com

22. "Now is the Time," June 22, 2006, by Joyce Howard

23. "Living A Lie–Life Without the Lord," May 26, 2006, by Joyce Howard

24. "Dialogue on Love," May 28, 2006, by Joyce Howard

25. Columbiere Retreat Center, Clarkston, MI, January 28, 1983, http://www.colombiere.com/

26. Poem: "I Grew Up Blamed," January 22, 1983, by Joyce Howard

27. Poem: "Gently Freeing," January 24, 1983, by Joyce Howard

28. Poem: "The Barriers of my Heart," January 26, 1983, by Joyce Howard

29. Poem: "Awakening," January 31, 1983, by Joyce Howard

30. Journal entry: "His Daughter," February 20, 1983, by Joyce Howard

31. *Covenant* definition, Microsoft Encarta College Dictionary, 2001, St. Martin's Press, New York

32. *Covenant with God* definition, Microsoft Encarta College Dictionary, 2001, St. Martin's Press, New York

33. *To agree in covenant* definition, Microsoft Encarta College Dictionary, 2001, St. Martin's Press, New York

34. Patricia Beall Gruits sermon, Shekinah Christian Church, Ann Arbor, MI, March 11, 2007

35. Thanksgiving letter, 2005, by Joyce Howard

36. Christmas letter, 2005, by Joyce Howard

37. Word to me about the college, May 9, 2006, by Joyce Howard

38. Word to me by MorningStar Prophetic Team, September 1, 2006, MorningStar Conference, Fort Mill, South Carolina, http://www.morningstarministries.org/

39. Word to me by MorningStar Prophetic Team, December 29, 2006, MorningStar Conference, Fort Mill, South Carolina, http://www.morningstarministries.org/

40. The Law of Conservation of Energy, NASA, Glenn Research Center website, http://www.grc.nasa.gov/WWW/K-12/airplane/thermo1f.html

41. *Pure* synonyms, Roget's Super Thesaurus, Marc McCutcheon, 1995, Thesaurus website, http://thesaurus.reference.com/

42. *Purify* synonyms, Roget's Super Thesaurus, Marc McCutcheon, 1995, Thesaurus website, http://thesaurus.reference.com/

43. Cleansing Stream Seminar and Retreat, held at City of Hope Church, Flint, MI; Now known as Ignite Flint Four Square Church, Pastor Todd Syruws, 4510 S. Dort Highway, Flint Mi.48507

44. "Grief Is A Choice," March 6, 2006, by Joyce Howard

45. Jim Bakker, *Jim Bakker Show*, Morningside Church, Branson, MO, http://www.jimbakkershow.com/

46. Billy Graham, Billy Graham Evangelistic Association, http://www.billygraham.org/

47. Franklin Graham, Samaritan's Purse International website, http://www.samaritanspurse.org/

48. Kenneth Copeland, April 25, 2006, Azusa Street Centennial, Crenshaw Christian Center, LA, CA, http://www.streamingfaith.com/directory/network.aspx?nsn=AZUSAODC

49. "The Story of My Nephew, Tom Howard, and Other Experiences of Intercession," January 6, 2007, by Joyce Howard

50. Ibid.

Called to Be Different

51. Ibid.

52. "It is written ..." found in Matthew 4:10 and Luke 4:10

53. *Stronghold* definition, Microsoft Encarta College Dictionary, 2001, St. Martin's Press, New York

54. Pastor Barbara J. Yoder, Shekinah Christian Church, Ann Arbor, MI, http://www.shekinahchurch.org/

55. *Bigotry* definition, Microsoft Encarta College Dictionary, 2001, St. Martin's Press, New York

56. *Hypocrisy* definition, Microsoft Encarta College Dictionary, 2001, St. Martin's Press, New York

57. *Hypocrite* definition, Microsoft Encarta College Dictionary, 2001, St. Martin's Press, New York

58. *Empiricism* definition, Microsoft Encarta College Dictionary, 2001, St. Martin's Press, New York

59. Metric system, FPSi (French Property, Services and Information Ltd.) website, http://www.france-property-and-information.com/metric-system-and-history.htm

60. *Gird* definition, Microsoft Encarta College Dictionary, 2001, St. Martin's Press, New York

61. Pat Robertson and The 700 Club, viewed on February 26, 1976, http://www.cbn.com/

62. "Get Ready Now," June 28, 2006, by Joyce Howard

63. Hurricane Katrina, August, 2005, Louisiana, Mississippi, Florida and entire Gulf Coast

64. "I Am Shaking," May 6, 2006, by Joyce Howard

65. "Judgment is Here," June 2, 2006, by Joyce Howard

66. "The Harvest has Begun," July 8, 2006, by Joyce Howard

67. *The Call Nashville*, Titans Stadium, Nashville, Tennessee, July 7, 2007, http://thecall.com/

68. Lou Engle, founder, TheCall website, http://thecall.com/

69. Patricia Beall Gruits sermon, March 11, 2007, Shekinah Christian Church, Ann Arbor, MI, http://www.shekinahchurch.org/

70. 40-Day Prayer Focus for *The Call Nashville*, Chuck D. Pierce, May 31, 2007, Glory of Zion International Ministries website, http://www.glory-of-zion.org/index.htm

71. *The Spirit of Baal* DVD series, Dutch Sheets, Destiny Bible School, DSM, Colorado Springs, CO, Dutch Sheets Ministries website, http://www.dutchsheets.org/index.cfm/pageid/263

72. Chuck D. Pierce, MIGAPN Conference, July 15, 2007, Shekinah Christian Church, Ann Arbor, MI, http://www.shekinahchurch.org/

73. *Time Changer* Movie, A Rich Christiano Film, 2002, Time Changer Movie website, http://www.timechangermovie.com/home.htm

74. Pastor Barbara J. Yoder sermon, September 16, 2007,

Shekinah Christian Church, Ann Arbor, MI, http://www.shekinahchurch.org/

75. Charles Darwin, About Darwin website, http://about-darwin.com/

76. "The Balfour Declaration," November 2, 1917, Israel Ministry of Foreign Affairs website, http://www.mfa.gov.il/MFA/Peace+Process/Guide+to+the+Peace+Process/The+Balfour+Declaration.htm

77. "The State of Israel is Born," April 1, 2008, Israel Ministry of Foreign Affairs website, http://www.mfa.gov.il/MFA/Facts+About+Israel/History/HISTORY-+The+State+of+Israel.htm

78. 40th Anniversary of the Reunification of Jerusalem, May 16, 2007, Israel Ministry of Foreign Affairs website, http://www.mfa.gov.il/MFA/Jerusalem+Capital+of+Israel/40th+Anniversary+of+the+Reunification+of+Jerusalem.htm

79. Azusa Street Revival, 1905, 312 Azusa Street website, http://www.azusastreet.org/

80. Oral Roberts Evangelistic Association website, http://www.orm.cc/?page_id=5; Billy Graham, Billy Graham Evangelistic Association, http://www.billygraham.org/; William Branham website, http://williambranham.com/

81. "Worldwide Renewal: The Charismatic Movement," Christianity Today Library website, http://www.ctlibrary.com/ch/1986/issue9/9105.html

Joyce A. Howard